Nick Vandome

iMac

in
easy steps

4th Edition

Updated for OS X Mountain Lion

In easy steps is an imprint of In Easy Steps Limited
4 Chapel Court · 42 Holly Walk · Leamington Spa
Warwickshire · United Kingdom · CV32 4YS
www.ineasysteps.com

Fourth Edition

Notice of Liability
Every effort has been made to ensure that this book contains accurate
and current information. However, In Easy Steps Limited and the
author shall not be liable for any loss or damage suffered by readers
as a result of any information contained herein.

Trademarks
Mac, iMac and OS X are registered trademarks of Apple Computer,
Inc. All other trademarks are acknowledged as belonging to their
respective companies.

In Easy Steps Limited supports The Forest Stewardship Council (FSC),
the leading international forest certification organisation. All our titles
that are printed on Greenpeace approved FSC certified paper carry the
FSC logo.

MIX
Paper from
responsible sources
FSC® C020837

Printed and bound in the United Kingdom

ISBN 978-1-84078-564-7

Contents

5 Finder   67

6 Navigating in Mountain Lion   87

7 iMac Apps   107

1 Introducing iMacs

The iMac is one of the most iconic computers of all time. This chapter introduces the latest version and details some of its main features.

About iMacs

In many ways, the iMac is the product that transformed the fortunes of Apple Computers and helped turn it into the world's most valuable technology company. The first iMac was introduced in 1998 and it was a major breakthrough in the world of personal computing. This was for two reasons: it was designed to be stylish rather than being just a functional beige box; and it combined the monitor and hard drive into one unit, as opposed to two separate ones.

Since its introduction, the iMac has gone through five major versions. Some of these involved a change of the processor which they use and some involved the physical design of the body of the iMac. But throughout this process, the principle of an all-in-one computer has remained.

The evolution of the iMac

The first appearance of the iMac, the iMac G3, was in 1998 with the brightly colored, all-in-one machines that made everyone in the computing world sit up and take notice. It was the first Mac computer to have a USB port, but not a floppy disk drive. The iMac was firmly aimed at the consumer computer market, rather than the professional market that was catered for with the Power Macintosh. However, a number of creative professionals, such as graphic designers and photographers, adopted the iMac, partly because of its eye-catching design.

The first iMacs came in a line of bright, translucent colors that were unique for the design of personal computers at the time:

iMac G4

The first major physical redesign of the iMac came in 2002 with the introduction of the iMac G4. This was more than a mere upgrade; it was another revolutionary design that quickly made its mark. It was still an all-in-one design, but the monitor and the hard drive were connected by an adjustable arm. The hard drive was contained within a white, dome-shaped base and the monitor, which was now LCD, could be moved and left in any position via the flexible arm. In contrast to the earlier models, the G4 came in white only and was the first Mac to use the OS X operating system that has now evolved into the current OS X Mountain Lion. The G4 iMac was discontinued in 2004, to be replaced by the G5 version.

Intel iMacs

The next redesign of the iMac was the G5. This was a more prosaic design, although still very stylish. The G5 had a PowerPC chip but in 2006 the processor for the iMac was changed to Intel processors. This continued across the range of Mac computers and the current iMacs are now powered by i5 or i7 Intel processors. The current iMacs also have a unibody aluminum body that is similar to other Apple products, such as the MacBook.

Don't forget

The latest version of the iMac is the neatest yet in terms of input devices. They are all wireless so there are no more cables to clutter up your desk.

iMac Specifications

There are currently two models of the iMac available, with 21.5-inch and 27-inch displays. There are two slightly different versions for each model and their specifications are:

iMac 21.5-inch

- 21.5-inch (diagonal) LED-backlit glossy widescreen TFT display with support for millions of colors

- 1920 x 1080 pixels resolution

- 2.5GHz, or 2.7GHz, quad-core Intel Core i5 processor with 6MB on-chip shared L3 cache

- 4GB (two 2GB) of 1333MHz DDR3 memory

- 500GB, or 1TB, (7200 rpm) hard drive storage

- AMD Radeon HD 6750M, or 6770M, graphics processor with 512MB of GDDR5 memory

- Built-in stereo speakers

- Built-in FaceTime HD camera

- One Thunderbolt port

- Mini DisplayPort output with support for DVI, VGA, and dual-link DVI (adapters sold separately)

- One FireWire 800 port

- Four USB 2.0 ports

- SDXC card slot

- Slot-loading 8x SuperDrive with 4x double-layer burning (DVD±R DL/DVD±RW/CD-RW)

- 802.11n Wi-Fi wireless networking; 2 IEEE 802.11a/b/g compatible

- Bluetooth 2.1 + EDR (Enhanced Data Rate) wireless technology

- Wireless Keyboard

- Magic Mouse or Magic Trackpad

iMac 27-inch

- 27-inch (diagonal) LED-backlit glossy widescreen TFT display with support for millions of colors

- 2560 by 1440 pixels resolution

- 2.7GHz, or 3.1GHz, quad-core Intel Core i5 processor with 6MB on-chip shared L3 cache (upgradeable to an i7 processor)

- 4GB (two 2GB) of 1333MHz DDR3 memory

- 1TB (7200 rpm) hard drive storage

- AMD Radeon HD 6770M, or 6970M, graphics processor with 512MB, or 1GB, of GDDR5 memory

- Built-in stereo speakers

- Built-in FaceTime HD camera

- Two Thunderbolt ports

- Mini DisplayPort output with support for DVI, VGA, and dual-link DVI (adapters sold separately)

- One FireWire 800 port

- Four USB 2.0 ports

- SDXC card slot

- Slot-loading 8x SuperDrive with 4x double-layer burning (DVD±R DL/DVD±RW/CD-RW)

- 802.11n Wi-Fi wireless networking; 2 IEEE 802.11a/b/g compatible

- Bluetooth 2.1 + EDR (Enhanced Data Rate) wireless technology

- Wireless Keyboard

- Magic Mouse or Magic Trackpad

Hot tip

By default, a new iMac comes with a Magic Mouse. If you want a Magic Trackpad instead, you have to specify this.

11

iMac Jargon Explained

Although the iMac is one of the most user-friendly computers on the market, it is unavoidable that there is some jargon connected with it:

- **Processor**. Also known as the central processing unit, or CPU, this refers to the processing of digital data as it is provided by apps on the computer. The more powerful the processor, the quicker the data is interpreted. As with the rest of Apple's computers, iMacs use Intel processors

- **Memory**. This closely relates to the processor and is also known as random-access memory, or RAM. Essentially, this type of memory manages the apps that are being run and the commands that are being executed. The greater the amount of memory there is, the quicker apps will run. With more RAM they will also be more stable and less likely to crash. In the current range of iMacs, memory is measured in gigabytes (GB) and both models have 4GB

- **Storage**. This refers to the amount of digital information the iMac can store. It is frequently referred to in terms of hard disk space and is measured in gigabytes or terabytes (TB). The minimum storage space on a standard iMac is 500GB on the 21.5-inch models and 1TB on the 27-inch models

- **Magic Mouse**. This is a wireless mouse that comes with all new iMacs. It connects via Bluetooth (page 13) and is a multi-touch device. This means that many operations such as scrolling through web pages or documents can be done on the surface of the mouse. There are no buttons on a Magic Mouse but different parts of it can be clicked on and they are assigned separate functions

Don't forget

Memory can be thought of as a temporary storage device, as it only keeps information about the currently-open apps. Storage is more permanent, as it keeps the information even when the iMac has been turned off.

- **Magic Trackpad**. This is an input device that performs the same functions as a trackpad on a MacBook laptop. As with the Magic Mouse it connects via Bluetooth and supports a wider range of Multi-Touch Gestures than the Magic Mouse. It also sits at the same angle as the iMac Wireless Keyboard so the two can sit comfortably side by side. (For an in-depth look at Multi-Touch Gestures on the Magic Trackpad and Magic Mouse, see Chapter Six.)

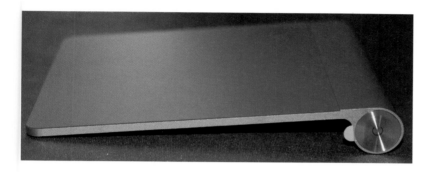

- **Wireless Keyboard**. New iMacs come with a Wireless Keyboard which, like the Magic Mouse and Magic Trackpad, connects via Bluetooth to the iMac

- **Graphics card**. This is a device that enables images, video and animations to be displayed on the iMac. It is also sometimes known as a video card. The faster the graphics card, the better the quality relevant media will be displayed at. In general, very fast graphics cards are really only needed for intensive multimedia applications, such as video games or videos. On an iMac this is the AMD Radeon HD Graphics card

- **Wireless**. This refers to an iMac's ability to connect wirelessly to a network, i.e. another computer or an Internet connection. In order to be able to do this, the iMac must have a wireless card, which enables it to connect to a network or high-speed Internet connection. This is known as the AirPort Extreme Wi-Fi wireless networking card

- **Bluetooth**. This is a radio technology for connecting devices wirelessly over a short distance. It can be used for items such as a wireless mouse, or for connecting to a device, such as an iPhone for downloading photos

Beware

The wireless input devices (keyboard, mouse and trackpad) are battery powered and can use up a lot of charge. It is a good idea to use rechargeable batteries to save having to buy a lot of new batteries.

Hot tip

To turn off the Magic Trackpad, press and hold the button on the side for a few seconds.

Don't forget

The iMac also has an ambient light sensor on the side of the body. This adjusts the display brightness, depending on the amount of available ambient light.

...cont'd

● **Ports**. These are the parts of an iMac where external devices can be plugged into, using a cable such as a USB, FireWire or Thunderbolt. They are located at the back of the iMac:

14

● **USB**. This is a method for connecting a variety of external devices, such as digital cameras, MP3 music players, scanners and printers

● **Ethernet**. This is for connecting an Ethernet cable to a router, for accessing the Internet, rather than doing it wirelessly

● **FireWire**. This is a similar method of data transfer to USB but is much faster. For this reason, it is generally used for devices that need to transfer larger amounts of data, such as digital video cameras

● **Thunderbolt**. This is a port for transferring data at high speeds, up to 12x faster than FireWire. It can also be used to attach a Thunderbolt Display monitor

● **CD/DVD players or re-writers**. On an iMac this is known as a SuperDrive, and is a thin slot on the side of the iMac. Discs are inserted by simply pushing them into the SuperDrive slot. The SuperDrive can be used to play music CDs, watch DVDs, copy data from CDs or DVDs, and copy data from your iMac onto CDs or DVDs

● **Webcam (FaceTime)**. This is a type of camera fitted into the top of the iMac and it can be used to take still photographs or communicate via video with other people. It works with the FaceTime app

Input Devices

iMacs have four options in terms of input devices:

- Wireless Keyboard
- Magic Mouse
- Magic Trackpad
- Standard mouse

Each item has its own preferences that can be selected from the System Preferences section. These preferences can be accessed by clicking on this button on the Dock at the bottom of the iMac screen (see Chapter Two for more details about System Preferences and Chapter Four for more details about the Dock).

Don't forget

Although new iMacs come with either a Magic Mouse or a Magic Trackpad they can also be used with a standard mouse.

Keyboard options

To access options for the Wireless Keyboard:

1 Access the System Preferences and click on the Keyboard button

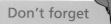

2 Click on the Keyboard tab to set the speed at which keystrokes are repeated and how long until the next one is active. There are also options for setting F key functionality and showing the keyboard settings in the Menu bar

3 Click on the Keyboard Shortcuts to set shortcut keys for accessing specific options and apps

...cont'd

Mouse options

There are different options for the mouse depending on whether it is a standard one or the Magic Mouse. Both are accessed in the same way:

1 Access the System Preferences and click on the Mouse button

2 For a Magic Mouse, click on the Point & Click tab for options for how you select items by clicking in different ways with the Magic Mouse

3 Click on the More Gestures tab for options for moving between pages and accessing full-screen apps and the Mission Control function

4 For a standard USB mouse, there are options for how quickly the cursor tracks the mouse and also the speed for double-clicking

Trackpad options

Options for the functioning of the Magic Trackpad can also be set within the System Preferences. To do this:

1 Access the System Preferences and click on the Trackpad button

2 Click on the Point & Click tab for options for how you select items by clicking, tapping and dragging in different ways with the Magic Trackpad

Don't forget

The battery level for all of the wireless devices is shown in their respective System Preferences windows.

3 Click on the Scroll & Zoom tab for options for moving around Web pages and documents

4 Click on the More Gestures tab for options for accessing additional items using the Magic Trackpad

17

Getting Started

When you start using your iMac there are a few steps to undertake before it is ready for normal use. These include powering on the iMac itself and also any input devices. You will then be able to proceed through the setup process. To do this:

1 Turn on the iMac by pressing this button on the bottom-right corner on the back of the iMac

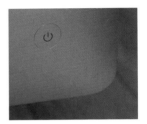

2 Turn on the Magic Trackpad and the Wireless Keyboard with this button at the front-right of the device

3 Turn on the Magic Mouse with this button underneath the device

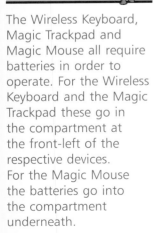
4 If you are using a Magic Trackpad, click on the bottom-left corner for single-click operations during setup

Once the iMac has been powered on there is a short setup process. This covers:

- Selecting the language you want to use on your iMac

- Finding the Wireless Keyboard and either the Magic Mouse or the Magic Trackpad

- Selecting the country in which you are located

- Selecting the country for the keyboard layout you want to use

- Detecting a Wi-Fi router, if you have one. If it is turned on the iMac will detect the router and you will be able to select it for network connection

- Entering an Apple ID, if you have one. If not, you can apply for one at this point

- Entering registration information for your iMac. This will be sent to Apple to confirm ownership of the iMac

- Entering information for your iMac computer account. This is used to administer the iMac

- Taking a photo for your user account. This is done by the built-in FaceTime camera

Once these steps have been completed the iMac is ready for use:

Hot tip

When the iMac is turned on it should automatically recognize the Wireless Keyboard and Magic Mouse/Magic Trackpad and 'pair' with them, i.e. associate them with the iMac. However, if this does not happen they can be set up within their respective System Preferences by clicking on the Set Up Bluetooth Keyboard/ Mouse/Trackpad button.

Hot tip

During the setup process you will be asked to enter a user name and a password. These are your administrator details, which allow you to change settings on your iMac. Take a note of your user name and password and keep it in a safe place, but away from the iMac itself.

Accessories

Adding accessories to your iMac can be a fun and productive way to get even more out of it. There are options for adding both hardware and software:

Hardware

- **Time Capsule**. This is a backup device that works wirelessly with the OS X backup app, Time Machine, to automatically back up everything on your iMac. It comes in 2TB or 3TB models

- **Apple Mini DisplayPorts**. These are connectors which enable you to connect to a larger monitor such as one of the Apple Cinema Displays or a TV

- **AirPort Express or Extreme Base Stations**. These are units which can be used to create a wireless network in your home or office. They connect to your iMac via its wireless card. The AirPort Express is smaller and therefore more portable so that it can be taken with you if you are traveling with a laptop. The AirPort Extreme is larger and more powerful but still relatively portable if needed

- **Pen drive**. This is a small device that can be used to copy data to and from your iMac. It connects via a USB port and is about the size of a packet of chewing gum

- **Cleaning material**. A lint-free cloth and screen cleaning spray can be used to clean your iMac's screen

Software

New software apps, or apps, can be downloaded directly from the Mac App Store. Some useful apps are:

- **iWork**. This is the Apple productivity suite which includes Pages for word processing, Numbers for data and spreadsheets, and Keynote for presentations

- **Aperture**. This is the high-end Apple image-editing app, the Mac equivalent to Photoshop

- **Logic Express**. This is a powerful app for creating and editing your own music

- **Final Cut Pro**. This is one of the best, and most powerful, apps for editing and publishing video

2 Around an iMac

This chapter looks at getting started with your iMac: from its keyboard functions to using CDs/DVDs and connecting external devices, such as printers and pen drives.

iMac Desktop

The opening view of an iMac is known as the Desktop. Items, such as apps and files, can be stored on the Desktop but, in general, it is best to try and keep it as clear as possible.

At the top of the Desktop is the Apple Menu and the Menu bar. This contains links to a collection of commonly-used menus and functions, such as Copy and Paste.

Don't forget

The menus on the Menu bar are looked at in detail in Chapter Five.

At the bottom of the Desktop is the Dock. This is a collection of icons that are shortcuts to frequently-used apps or folders.

One of the items on the Dock is the Finder. This can be used to access the main area for apps, folders and files and also organize the way you work on your iMac.

Apple Menu

The Apple Menu is accessed from the Apple symbol at the left-hand side of the Menu bar:

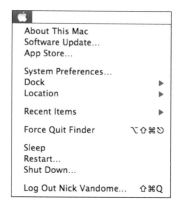

The options on the Apple Menu are:

- **About this Mac**. This provides general information about the processor, the amount of memory and the OS X version

- **Software Update.** This takes you to the Updates section of the App Store

- **App Store**. This can be used to access the online Mac App Store for downloading apps

- **System Preferences**. This is a shortcut to System Preferences

- **Dock**. This can be used to access settings for the Dock

- **Location**. This lists available network locations

- **Recent Items**. This displays the items you have most recently used and viewed

- **Force Quit**. This can be used to manually quit an app that has frozen or will not close

- **Sleep**. This puts the iMac into a state of hibernation

- **Restart**. This closes down the iMac and restarts it

- **Shut Down**. This shuts down the iMac

- **Log Out**. This logs out the current user

Hot tip

Force Quit can be used to close down an app that is frozen or is not responding.

Keyboard Buttons

As shown on page 23, the Apple Menu has options for Sleep, Restart and Shut Down. Sleep saves your current session and puts the iMac into a state of hibernation. This is useful if your iMac is going to be inactive for a period but you do not want to close it down.

Shortcut keys can also be used to put the iMac to sleep.

To do this, press the Alt and Command (cmd) keys and the Eject key simultaneously. (The Alt and Command keys are located on the left-hand side of the space bar and the Eject key is at the top-right of the keyboard.)

Fn (Function) Keys

An iMac keyboard has a number of keys that can be used for shortcuts or specific functions. Four of them are located to the left of the space bar. They are (from left to right):

- **The Function key**. This can be used to activate the function (F) keys at the top of the keyboard. To activate the operation of a function key, press it while holding down the Fn key

- **The Control key**. This can be used to access contextual menus

- **The Alt (Option) key**. This is frequently used in conjunction with the Command key to perform specific tasks, such as above with Sleep

- **The Command key**. As above

Don't forget

Restart is most frequently used if there is a problem on your iMac, such as a frozen app, and you want to turn it off and then back on again to try and resolve the issue.

Don't forget

Contextual menus are ones that have actions that are specific to the item being viewed.

24

At the top of the keyboard there are keys for changing some of the settings on your iMac. These are (from left to right):

- F1: Decrease brightness

- F2: Increase brightness

- F3: Show all open windows (Mission Control)

- F4: Show/Hide the Launchpad (see Chapter Seven)

- F7: Rewind a video

- F8: Play/Pause a video

- F9: Fast forward a video

- F10: Mute volume

- F11: Decrease volume (use with the Fn key to display the iMac desktop)

- F12: Increase volume (use with the Fn key to activate the Dashboard set of widgets)

- Eject button. Remove CDs/DVDs from the SuperDrive

Don't forget

By default, the F keys operate without having to simultaneously press the Fn key. If you want to use the Fn key in conjunction with the F keys, this can be specified in the System Preferences. To do this, open System Preferences and click on the Keyboard button. Under the Keyboard tab, check on the box that says "Use all F keys as standard function keys".

System Preferences

In OS X there are preferences that can be set for just about every aspect of the app. This gives you great control over how the interface looks and how the operating system functions. To access System Preferences:

Click on this icon on the Dock or from the Applications folder in the Finder

Personal preferences

General. Options for the overall look of buttons, menus, windows and scroll bars.

Desktop & Screen Saver. This can be used to change the desktop background and the screen saver.

Dock. Options for the way the Dock looks and functions.

Mission Control This gives you a variety of options for managing all of your open windows and apps.

Language & Text. Options for the language used on the computer.

Security &Privacy. This enables you to secure your Home folder with a master password, for added security.

Spotlight. This can be used to specify settings for the OS X search facility, Spotlight.

Notifications. This can be used to set up how you are notified about items such as email, messages and software updates.

Hardware preferences

CDs & DVDs. Options for what action is taken when you insert CDs and DVDs.

Displays. Options for the screen display, such as resolution.

Energy Saver. Options for when the computer is inactive.

Keyboard. Options for how the keyboard functions and also keyboard shortcuts.

Mouse. Options for how the mouse functions.

Trackpad. Options for when you are using a trackpad.

Don't forget

For more information about the Dock, see Chapter Four, and for the Finder, Chapter Five.

Print & Scan. Options for selecting printers and scanners.

Sound. Options for adding sound effects and playing and recording sound.

Internet & Wireless preferences
iCloud. Options for the online iCloud service.

Mail, Contacts & Calendars. This can be used to set up contacts on your Mac, using a variety of online services.

Network. This can be used to specify network settings for linking two or more computers together. This is covered in more detail in Chapter Eleven.

Bluetooth. Options for attaching Bluetooth wireless devices

Sharing. This can be used to specify how files are shared over a network. This is also covered in Chapter Eleven.

System preferences
Users & Groups. This can be used to allow different users to create their own accounts for use on the same computer.

Parental Controls. This can be used to limit access to the computer and various online functions.

Date & Time. Options for changing the computer's date and time to time zones around the world.

Software Update. This can be used to specify how software updates are handled. It connects to the App Store to access the available updates.

Dictation & Speech. Options for using speakable commands to control the computer.

Time Machine. This can be used to configure and set up the OS X backup facility.

Accessibility. This can be used to set options for users who have difficulty with viewing text on screen, hearing commands, using the keyboard or using the mouse.

Startup Disk. This can be used to specify the disk from which your computer starts up. This is usually the OS X volume.

Hot tip

The General tab within the Security & Privacy preferences can be used to specify whether you require a password after the iMac has been woken from sleep or the screensaver has been activated. For security reasons it is recommended that it is activated, but if you know you will be the only person who has access to the iMac you can check this off.

27

Connecting a Printer

OS X Mountain Lion makes the printing process as simple as possible, partly by being able to automatically install new printers as soon as they are connected to your iMac. However, it is also possible to install printers manually. To do this:

1. Open the System Preferences folder and click on the Print & Scan button

Print & Scan

2. Currently-installed printers are displayed in the Printers List. Click here to add a new printer and click on either the Add Other Printer or Scanner link or any currently-available printers

Add Other Printer or Scanner...

Nearby Printers
Dell Laser Printer 1720dn

3. OS X Mountain Lion loads the required printer driver (if it does not have a specific one it will try to use a generic one)

Setting up 'Dell Laser Printer 1720dn...'
The software for this printer is currently unavailable. Would you like to use generic software for printing?

Cancel   Use Generic

4. The details about the printer are available in the Print & Scan window

Printers
Dell Laser Printer 172...
Idle, Last Used

Dell Laser Printer 1720dn

Open Print Queue...
Options & Supplies...

Location:
Kind: Generic PostScript Printer
Status: Idle

5. Once a printer has been installed, documents can be printed by selecting File>Print from the Menu bar. Print settings can be set at this point and they can also be set by selecting File>Page/Print Setup from the Menu bar in most apps

CD and DVD SuperDrive

The SuperDrive on an iMac can be used to copy data from a CD or DVD onto the hard drive, or vice versa. As with many of the functions of an iMac there are settings that can be applied within the System Preferences. To do this:

Hardware

CDs & DVDs

1 Open System Preferences and click on this icon under the Hardware section

2 There are various options for what happens when you insert blank CDs/DVDs and also for music, picture and video CDs/DVDs

Don't forget

The SuperDrive slot is located on the right-hand side of the iMac.

29

3 If you insert a blank CD or DVD the following window appears automatically. The Action box offers options for what you want to do with the CD or DVD. Click on the OK button to select an action or click on the Ignore button if you do not want to use any of these actions

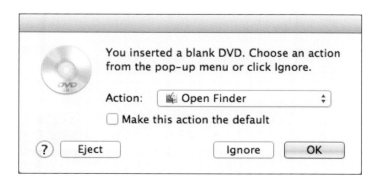

External Drives

Attaching external drives is an essential part of mobile computing, whether it is to back up data as you are traveling or for downloading photos and other items. On iMacs, external drives are displayed on the Desktop once they have been attached and they can then be used for the required task. To do this:

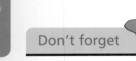
1 Attach the external drive. This is usually done with a USB cable. Once it has been attached it is shown on the Desktop

2 The drive is shown under the Devices section of the Finder

3 Perform the required task for the external drive (such as copying files or folders onto it from the hard drive of your iMac)

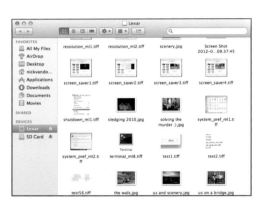

4 External drives have to be ejected properly, not just pulled out or removed. To do this, click on this button next to the drive in the Finder window, or drag its icon on the Desktop over the Trash icon on the Dock. This will then change into an Eject icon

3 iMac Basics

Mountain Lion is the latest operating system for the iMac. It is enjoyable to use and has a raft of features that transform a number of computing functions. This chapter introduces Mountain Lion and shows how to get started with it.

About OS X Mountain Lion

OS X Mountain Lion is the eighth version (10.8) of the operating system for Apple computers; the iMac, MacBook, Mac Mini and Mac Pro. When OS X (pronounced 'ten') was first introduced it was a major breakthrough in terms of ease of use and stability. It is based on the UNIX programming language, which is a very stable and secure operating environment and ensures that OS X is one of the most stable consumer operating systems that has ever been designed. More importantly for the user, it is also one of the most stylish and user-friendly operating systems available.

Through the previous seven versions of OS X it has been refined and improved in terms of both performance and functionality. This process continues with OS X Mountain Lion, which further develops the innovations introduced by its predecessor, Lion.

When OS X Lion was introduced, in 2011, it had a range of innovative functions that were inspired by Apple's mobile devices: iPhone, iPod Touch and iPad. The two main areas where the functionality of the mobile devices has been transferred to the desktop and laptop operating system are:

- The way apps can be downloaded and installed. Instead of using a disc, OS X Mountain Lion utilizes the Mac App Store to provide apps, which can be installed in a couple of simple steps

- Options for navigating around pages and applications on a Trackpad or a Magic Mouse. Instead of having to use a mouse or a traditional laptop trackpad, OS X Mountain Lion allows Multi-Touch Gestures that provide a range of ways for accessing apps and web pages and navigating around them

OS X Mountain Lion takes the work of OS X Lion even further, by adding more features that initially appeared on the iPad. These include the iMessage service, Notification Center, Reminders, Notes and the Game Center. There are also additions to the iCloud service that keep all of your content and devices synchronized and up to date.

OS X Lion was a genuinely revolutionary operating system in terms of the way in which people work and interact with their Macs. OS X Mountain Lion continues this work and takes it to the next level of power and functionality.

Don't forget

UNIX is an operating system that has traditionally been used for large commercial mainframe computers. It is renowned for its stability and ability to be used within different computing environments.

Don't forget

Mountain Lion has a Power Nap function that updates items from the online iCloud service even when an iMac is in sleep mode. This can be set up by checking on the Wake for Network Access option in the Energy Saver section of System Preferences.

Installing Mountain Lion

When it comes to installing OS X Moutain Lion you do not need to worry about an installation disk; it can be downloaded and installed directly from the online Mac App Store. New iMacs will have Mountain Lion installed but if you want to install it on an existing iMac you will need to have a minimum requirement of:

- OS X Snow Leopard (version 10.6.8 or later) or OS X Lion

- Intel Core 2 Duo, Core i3, Core i5, Core i7, or Xeon processor

- 2Gb of memory

If your iMac meets these requirements, you can download and install OS X Mountain Lion as follows:

1 Click on this icon on the Dock to access the App Store

2 Locate the Mountain Lion icon and click on the Buy button

3 Once Mountain Lion has been downloaded, click on this button to start the installation process

4 Follow the installation screens including one for where OS X Mountain Lion is installed (this is usually the Mac Hard Disk)

Don't forget

If you already have OS X Lion, you can download and install Mountain Lion directly from the App Store. If you are using Snow Leopard you will have to upgrade to version 10.6.8 before you can install Mountain Lion.

Hot tip

If you ever need to do so, it is possible to reinstall OS X Mountain Lion. To do this you will need an Internet connection. Once this has been checked, select Restart from the Apple menu. When the iMac restarts, hold down the Command and R keys simultaneously. In the Mac OS X Utilities window, select Reinstall Mac OS X, click on the Continue button and follow the on-screen instructions.

The OS X Environment

The first most noticeable element about OS X is its elegant user interface. This has been designed to create a user friendly graphic overlay to the UNIX operating system at the heart of OS X and it is a combination of rich colors and sharp, original graphics. The main elements that make up the initial OS X environment are:

Apple menu   Menu bar   Windows

The Dock   Desktop

Hot tip

The Dock is designed to help make organizing and opening items as quick and easy as possible. For a detailed look at the Dock, see Chapter Four.

The Apple menu is standardized throughout OS X, regardless of the app in use

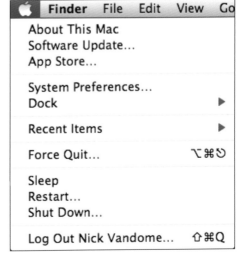

Aqua Interface

The name given by Apple to its OS X interface is Aqua. This describes the graphical appearance of the operating system. Essentially, it is just the cosmetic appearance of the elements within the operating system, but they combine to give OS X a rich visual look and feel. Some of the main elements of the Aqua interface are:

Menus

Menus in OS X contain commands for the operating system and any relevant apps. If there is an arrow next to a command it means there are subsequent options for the item:

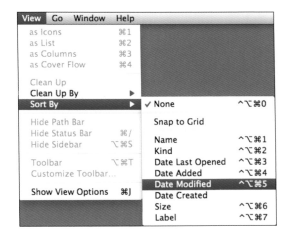

Window buttons

These appear in any open OS X window and can be used to manipulate the window.

Option buttons

Whenever a dialog box with separate options is accessed, OS X highlights the suggested option with a pulsing blue button. This can be accepted by clicking on it or by pressing Enter. If you do not want to accept this option, click on another button in the dialog box.

About Your iMac

When you buy a new iMac you will almost certainly check the technical specifications before you make a purchase. Once you have your iMac, there will be times when you will want to view these specifications again, such as the version of OS X in use, the amount of memory and the amount of storage. This can be done through the About This Mac option that can be accessed from the Apple Menu. To do this:

1 Click on the Apple Menu and click on the About This Mac link

2 The About This Mac window has information about the version of OS X, the processor, the memory and the Startup Disk being used

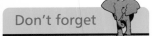
Don't forget

For more information about Software Updates, see Chapter Twelve.

3 Click on the Software Update... button to see available software updates for your iMac

4 Click on the More Info... button to view more About This Mac options

Overview

This gives additional general information about your iMac:

1 Click on the Overview button

2 This window contains additional information such as the type of graphics card and the Serial Number

3 Click on the System Report... button to view full details about the hardware and software on your iMac

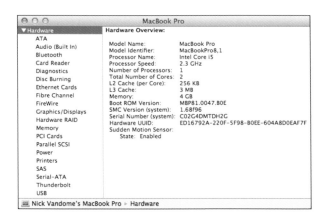

4 Click on the Check for Updates... button to view available software updates for your iMac

...cont'd

Display information
This gives information about your iMac's display:

1 Click on the Displays button **Displays**

2 This window
contains
information about
your display
including the type,
size, resolution
and graphics card

3 Click on
the Displays
Preferences...
button to view options for changing the display's
resolution, brightness and color

Displays Preferences...

Storage information
This contains information about your iMac's physical and
removable storage:

Don't forget

For more information
about changing the
resolution, see page 42.

1 Click on the Storage button **Storage**

2 This window
contains
information about
the used and
available storage
on your hard disk
and also options
for writing various
types of CDs and
DVDs

3 Click on the Disk Utility... button to view options for repairing problems on your iMac

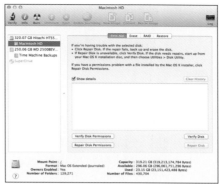

Memory information

This contains information about your iMac's memory, which is used to run OS X and also the applications on your computer:

1 Click on the Memory button

2 This window contains information about the memory chips that are in your iMac

3 Click on the Memory Upgrade Instructions if you want to upgrade your memory chips

4 A page on the Apple website gives instructions for upgrading memory chips for different models of Macs

Notifications

The Notification Center option provides a single location to view all of your emails, messages, updates and alerts. It appears at the top right-hand corner of the screen. The items that appear in Notifications are set up within System Preferences. To do this:

1 Open System Preferences and click on this icon

2 The items that will appear in the Notification Center are listed here. Click on an item to select it and set its notification options

Twitter feeds can also be set up to appear in the Notifications Center, as will Facebook updates, when this facility becomes available.

3 To disable an item so that it does not appear in the Notification Center, select it as above and check off the Show in Notification Center box

Viewing Notifications

Notifications appear in the Notification Center. The way they appear can be determined in the System Preferences:

1 Select an alert style. A banner alert comes up on the screen and then disappears after a few seconds

2 The Alerts option shows the notification and it stays on screen until dismissed (such as this one for reminders)

3 Click on this button in the top right-hand corner of the screen to view all of the items in the Notification Center. Click on it again to hide the Notification Center

4 In the Notifications Center, click on one to open it or view more details about it

41

The Notification Center can also be displayed with a Trackpad or Magic Trackpad by dragging with two fingers from right to left, starting from the far-right edge.

Don't forget

Software updates also appear in the Notifications Center, when they are available.

Changing the Resolution

For most computer users the size at which items are displayed on the screen is a crucial issue: if items are too small this can make them hard to read and lead to eye strain; too large and you have to spend a lot of time scrolling around to see everything.

The size of items on the screen is controlled by the screen's resolution, i.e. the number of colored dots displayed in an area of the screen. The higher the resolution the smaller the items on the screen, the lower the resolution the larger the items. To change the screen resolution:

1 Click on this button in the System Preferences folder

Displays

Don't forget

A higher resolution makes items appear sharper on the screen, even though they appear physically smaller.

2 Click on the Display tab

Display

3 Click on the Best for built-in display button to let your iMac select the most appropriate resolution

Display	Color

Resolution: ⦿ Best for built-in display
○ Scaled

Brightness: ──────────○──────
☑ Automatically adjust brightness

4 Drag this slider to change the screen brightness. Check on the box to have this done automatically

Don't forget

The screen background and screen saver can also be set in the System Preferences, using the Desktop & Screen Saver preferences.

5 Click on the Scaled button and select a resolution setting to change the overall screen resolution

Display	Color

Resolution: ○ Best for built-in display
⦿ Scaled

1280 × 800
1152 × 720
1024 × 768
1024 × 640
800 × 600

6 Click on the Color tab to select options for using different color profiles and also calibrating your monitor

Color

Accessibility

In all areas of computing it is important to give as many people access to the system as possible. This includes users with visual impairments and also people who have problems using the mouse and keyboard. In OS X this is achieved through the functions of the Accessibility System Preferences. To use these:

1 Click on this button in the System Preferences folder

2 Click on the Display button for options for changing the display colors, contrast and increasing the cursor size

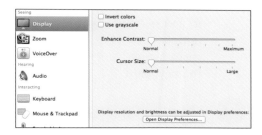

3 Click on the Zoom button for options to zoom in on the screen

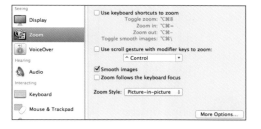

4 Click on the VoiceOver button to enable VoiceOver, which provides a spoken description of what is on the screen

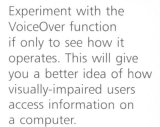

Don't forget

Experiment with the VoiceOver function if only to see how it operates. This will give you a better idea of how visually-impaired users access information on a computer.

...cont'd

5 Click on the Audio button to select an on-screen flash for alerts and how sound is played

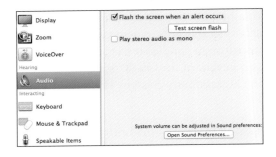

6 Click on the Keyboard button to access options for customizing the keyboard

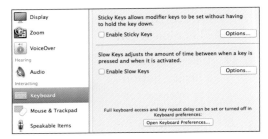

44

7 Click on the Mouse & Trackpad button to access options for customizing these devices

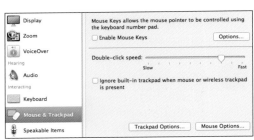

8 Click on the Speakable Items button to select options for using spoken commands

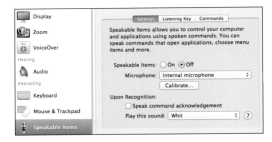

9 Click on this button to enable assistive technology such as screen readers

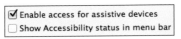

The Spoken Word

Mountain Lion not only has numerous options for adding text to documents, emails and messages; it also has a dictation function so that you can speak what you want to appear on screen. To set up and use the dictation feature:

1 Click on this button in the System Preferences folder

2 By default, Dictation is Off

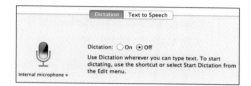

3 Click on the On button to enable Dictation

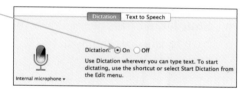

Hot tip

Punctuation can be added with the dictation function, by speaking commands such as 'comma' or 'question mark'. These will then be converted into the appropriate symbols.

45

4 Click on the Enable Dictation button

5 Once Dictation has been turned On, it can be accessed in relevant apps by selecting Edit>Start Dictation from the menu bar

6 Start talking when the microphone icon appears. Click Done when you have finished recording your text

7 Click on the Text to Speech tab to make selections for dictation

Shutting Down

The Apple menu (which can be accessed by clicking on the Apple icon at the top left corner of the desktop or any subsequent OS X window) has been standardized in OS X. This means that it has the same options regardless of the app in which you are working. This has a number of advantages, not least is the fact that it makes it easier to shut down your iMac. When shutting down, there are three options that can be selected:

- **Sleep**. This puts the iMac into hibernation mode, i.e. the screen goes blank and the hard drive becomes inactive. This state is maintained until the mouse is moved or a key is pressed on the keyboard. This then wakes up the iMac and it is ready to continue work

- **Restart**. This closes down the iMac and then restarts it again. This can be useful if you have added new software and your computer requires a restart to make it active

- **Shut Down**. This closes down the iMac completely once you have finished working

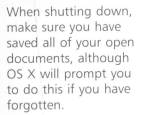

Don't forget

When shutting down, make sure you have saved all of your open documents, although OS X will prompt you to do this if you have forgotten.

Don't forget

OS X Mountain Lion has a Resume function where your iMac opens up in the same state as when you shut it down. See Chapter Four for details.

46

Click here to access the Apple menu

Click here to access one of the Shut Down options

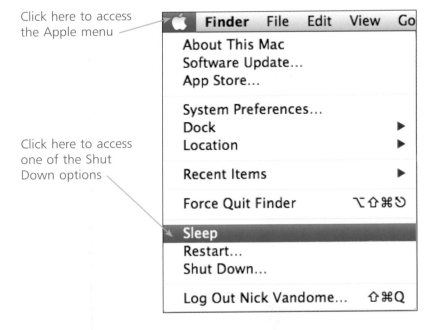

4 Getting Up and Running

This chapter looks at some of the essential features of Mountain Lion. These include the Dock for organizing and accessing the elements of the computer, the system preferences for the way the computer looks and operates and items for arranging folders and files. It also introduces the online sharing service, iCloud.

Introducing the Dock

The Dock is one of the main organizational elements of OS X. Its main function is to help organize and access apps, folders and files. In addition, with its rich translucent colors and elegant graphical icons, it also makes an aesthetically pleasing addition to the desktop. The main things to remember about the Dock are:

- It is divided into two: apps go on the left of the dividing line; all other items go on the right

- It can be edited in just about any way you choose

By default the Dock appears at the bottom of the screen

Apps go here   Dividing line   Open items

If an app window is closed, the app remains open and the window is placed within the app icon on the Dock. If an item is minimized it goes on the right of the Dock dividing line.

Setting Dock Preferences

As with most elements of OS X, the Dock can be modified in numerous ways. This can affect both the appearance of the Dock and the way it operates. To set Dock preferences:

1 Select Apple Menu>Dock from the Menu bar

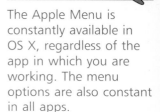

Turn Hiding On	⌥⌘D
Turn Magnification On	
Position on Left	
✓ Position on Bottom	
Position on Right	
Dock Preferences...	

2 Select the general preferences here

Dock Preferences...

3 Click here to access more Dock preferences (below)

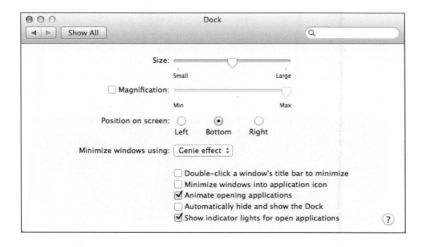

Hot tip

The Apple Menu is constantly available in OS X, regardless of the app in which you are working. The menu options are also constant in all apps.

Beware

You will not be able to make the Dock size too large so that some of the icons would not be visible on the desktop. By default, the Dock is resized so that everything is always visible.

49

...cont'd

The Dock Preferences allow you to change its size, orientation, the way icons appear and effects for when items are minimized:

The "Position on screen" options enable you to place the Dock on the left, right or bottom of the screen

The Dock cannot be moved by dragging it physically, this can only be done in the Dock Preferences window.

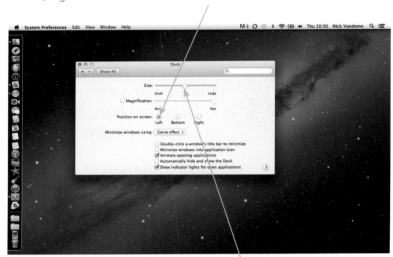

When the cursor is moved over an item in the Dock, the name of that item is displayed above it.

Drag the Dock Size slider to increase or decrease the size of the Dock

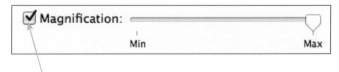

Check on the Magnification box and drag the slider to determine the size to which icons are enlarged when the cursor is moved over them

The effects that are applied to items when they are minimized is one of the features of OS X (it is not absolutely necessary but it sums up the Apple ethos of trying to enhance the user experience as much as possible).

The Genie effect shrinks the item to be minimized like a genie going back into its lamp

Open windows can also be minimized by double-clicking on their title bar (the thinly-lined bar at the top of the window, next to the three window buttons.)

Manual resizing

In addition to changing the size of the Dock by using the Dock Preference dialog box, it can also be resized manually:

Drag vertically on the Dock dividing line to increase or decrease its size

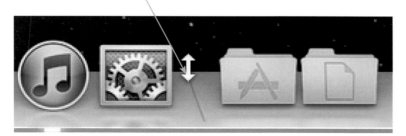

Stacks on the Dock

Stacking items

To save space on the Dock it is possible to add folders to the Dock, from where their contents can be accessed. This is known as Stacks. By default, Stacks for documents and downloaded files are created on the Dock. To use Stacks:

1 Stacked items are placed on the right of the Dock dividing line

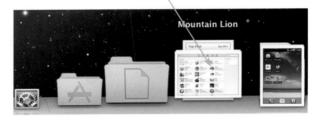

To create a new Stack, drag a folder to the right-hand side of the Dock, i.e. to the right of the dividing line.

2 Click on a Stack to view its contents

3 Stacks can be viewed as a grid, or

4 As a fan, depending on the number of items it contains, or

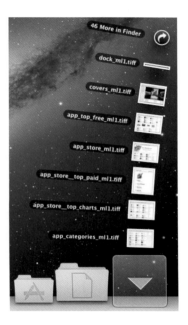

5 As a list. Click on a folder to view its contents within a Stack. Click on files to open them in their relevant app

6 To create a new Stack, drag a folder onto the Dock. Any new items that are added to the folder will also be visible through the Stack

Dock Menus

One of the features of the Dock is that it can display contextual menus for selected items. This means that it shows menus with options that are applicable to the item that is being accessed. This can only be done when an item has been opened.

1 Click and hold here to display an item's individual menu

2 Click on Show in Finder to see where the item is located on your computer

Working with Dock Items

Adding items

As many items as you like can be added to the Dock; the only restriction is the size of monitor in which to display all of the Dock items (the size of the Dock can be reduced to accommodate more icons but you have to be careful that all of the icons are still legible). To add items to the Dock:

Locate the required item and drag it onto the Dock. All of the other icons move along to make space for the new one

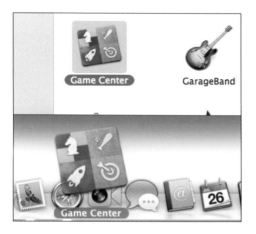

Don't forget

Icons on the Dock are shortcuts to the related item, rather than the item itself, which remains in its original location.

Keep in Dock

Every time you open a new app, its icon will appear in the Dock for the duration that the program is open, even if it has not previously been put in the Dock. If you then decide that you would like to keep it in the Dock, you can do so as follows:

Beware

You can add as many items as you like to the Dock, but it will automatically shrink to display all of its items if it becomes too big for the available space.

1 Click and hold on the icon underneath an open app

2 Click on Keep In Dock to ensure the app remains in the Dock when it is closed

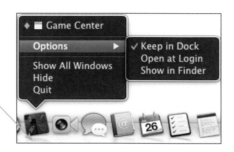

...cont'd

Removing items

Any item, except the Finder, can be removed from the Dock. However, this does not remove it from your computer, it just removes the shortcut for accessing it. You will still be able to locate it in its folder on your hard drive and, if required, drag it back onto the Dock. To remove items from the Dock:

Drag it away from the Dock and release. The item disappears in a satisfying puff of smoke to indicate that it has been removed. All of the other icons then move up to fill in the space

Removing open apps

You can remove an app from the Dock, even if it is open and running. To do this:

1 Drag an app off the Dock while it is running. Initially the icon will remain on the Dock because the app is still open

2 When the app is closed its icon will be removed from the Dock (unless Keep in Dock has been selected from the item's Dock menu)

Trash

The Trash folder is a location for placing items that you do not want to use anymore. However, when items are placed in the Trash, they are not removed from your computer. This requires another command, as the Trash is really a holding area before you decide you want to remove items permanently. The Trash can also be used for ejecting removable disks attached to your iMac.

Sending items to the Trash

Items can be sent to the Trash by dragging them from the location in which they are stored:

1 Drag an item over the Trash icon to place it in the Trash folder

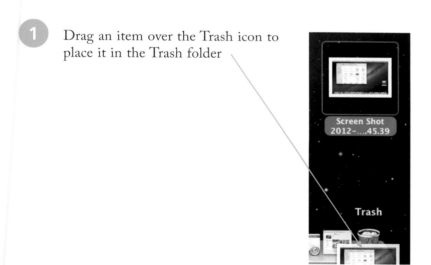

Don't forget

Items can also be sent to the Trash by selecting them and then selecting File>Move to Trash from the Menu bar.

2 Click once on the Trash icon on the Dock to view its contents

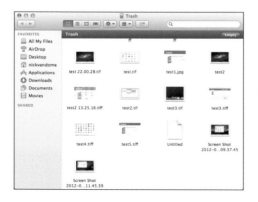

Don't forget

All of the items within the Trash can be removed in a single command: Select Finder>Empty Trash from the Menu bar to remove all of the items in the Trash folder.

About iCloud

Cloud computing is an attractive proposition and one that has gained greatly in popularity in recent years. As a concept, it consists of storing your content on an external computer server. This not only gives you added security in terms of backing up your information, it also means that the content can then be shared over a variety of mobile devices.

iCloud is Apple's consumer cloud computing product that consists of online services such as email, a calendar, contacts and saving documents. iCloud provides users with a way to save their files and content to the online service and then use them across their Apple devices such as other Mac computers, iPhones, iPads and iPod Touches.

About iCloud

iCloud can be set up from this icon with System Preferences:

You can use iCloud to save and share the following:

- Music

- Photos

- Documents

- Apps

- Books

- Backups

- Contacts and calendars

When you save an item to the iCloud it automatically pushes it to all of your other compatible devices; you do not have to manually sync anything, iCloud does it all for you.

Don't forget

The standard iCloud service is free and this includes an iCloud email address and 5GB of online storage.

Don't forget

There is also a version of iCloud for Windows.

Setting up iCloud

To use iCloud with Mountain Lion you need to first have an
Apple ID. This is a service you can register for to be able to access
a range of Apple facilities, including iCloud. You can register
with an email address and a password. When you first start using
iCloud you will be prompted for your Apple ID details. If you do
not have an Apple ID you can apply for one at this point:

1 Sign in with your
Apple ID, or

2 Click on this button to
create a new one

Setting up iCloud
To use iCloud

1 Open System Preferences and click on the
iCloud button

2 Check on
the items you
want included
within
iCloud. All of
these items
will be backed
up and shared
across all of
your Apple
devices

Using iCloud

Once iCloud has been set up in System Preferences there is relatively little that needs to be done. iCloud will take care of things in the background and back up and share all of the items that have been specified. For instance, when you create a note or a reminder it will be saved by iCloud and made available to any other Apple devices that are iCloud-enabled. Photos and documents can also be shared via iCloud.

Sharing photos

Photos can be shared via iCloud using the iPhoto app:

1 When iCloud is active, a Photo Stream folder is created in iPhoto. Click on this to view its contents

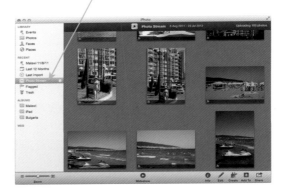

2 All of the photos in the Photo Stream will be available in other iCloud-enabled devices. Similarly, you will be able to view the Photo Streams from your other devices

Sharing documents

The latest versions of the Apple productivity apps (Pages, Numbers or Keynote) are optimized for use with iCloud. This means that if you create a presentation or report on, for instance, an iPad, you can also open it on a Mac running Mountain Lion (as long as you have the same apps). To share documents:

1 In the iCloud System Preferences, make sure that the Documents & Data option is checked On

2 Open one of the Apple productivity apps, such as Pages

3 Click on the iCloud button to view which documents are available in the iCloud. Click on the On My Mac button to see which documents are just on your iMac

4 Open and edit a document from the iCloud. The edited document will then be available on other iCloud-enabled devices

5 If you create a new document on your iMac, you can move it to the iCloud. Click here next to the document's name and click on Move To...

6 Make sure that iCloud is selected in the Where box and click on the Save button

Desktop Items

If required, the Desktop can be used to store apps and files. However, the Finder (see Chapter Five) does such a good job of organizing all of the elements within your computer that the Desktop is rendered largely redundant, unless you feel happier storing items here. The Desktop also displays any removable disks that are connected to your computer:

If a removable disk is connected to your computer, double-click the Desktop icon to view its contents

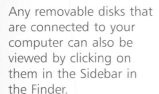
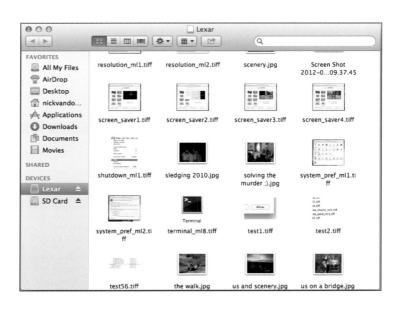

Ejecting Items

If you have removable disks attached to your Mac it is essential to be able to eject them quickly and easily. In OS X there are two ways in which this can be done:

1 In the Finder, click on the icon to the right of the name of the removable disk

2 On the Desktop, drag the disk icon over the Trash. This turns the Trash icon into the Eject icon and the disk will be ejected

SD Card

Lexar
Lexar

Don't forget

Items can also be ejected by selecting File>Eject from the Finder menu.

3 Some disks, such as CDs and DVDs are physically ejected when either of these two actions are performed. Other disks, such as pen drives, have to be removed manually once they have been ejected by OS X. If the disk is not ejected first the following warning message will appear:

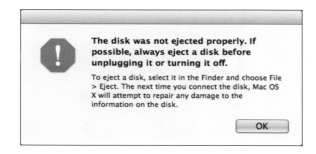

The disk was not ejected properly. If possible, always eject a disk before unplugging it or turning it off.

To eject a disk, select it in the Finder and choose File > Eject. The next time you connect the disk, Mac OS X will attempt to repair any damage to the information on the disk.

OK

Auto Save and Versions

One of the biggest causes of frustration when working with computers is if they crash and all of your unsaved work is lost. Luckily, with OS X Mountain Lion, losing unsaved material is now a thing of the past as it includes an Auto Save function that saves work in the background as you go along. This means that you do not have to worry about having unsaved documents.

Another function within Auto Save is Versions, which enables you to revert back to previous versions of a document. To do this:

1 Create a document with content

2 Select File>Save from the Menu bar

3 Edit the file

4 Click on the file name and select Browse All Versions...

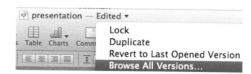

5 The current version is shown on the left-hand side and the previous versions on the right

6 Click on a previous version

7 Click on the Restore button

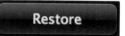

8 The previous version is restored as the current document

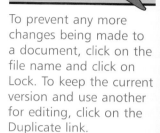

Hot tip

To prevent any more changes being made to a document, click on the file name and click on Lock. To keep the current version and use another for editing, click on the Duplicate link.

Resuming

One of the chores of computing is that when you close down your computer you have to first close down all of your open documents and apps and then open them all again when you turn your machine back on. However, OS X Mountain Lion has an innovative feature that allows you to continue working exactly where you left off, even if you turn off your computer. To do this:

1 Before you close down, all of your open documents and apps will be available as shown

2 Select the Shut Down or Restart option from the Apple menu

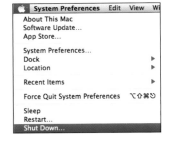

3 Make sure this box is checked on (this will ensure that all of your items will appear as before once the Mac is closed down and then opened again)

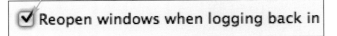

4 Confirm the Shut Down or Restart command

5 Finder

The principal way for moving around OS X Mountain Lion is the Finder. This enables you to access items and organize your apps, folders and files. This chapter looks at how to use the Finder and how to get the most out of this powerful tool. It covers accessing items through the Finder, how to customize the interface and numerous options for working with folders in OS X.

Working with the Finder

If you were only able to use one item on the Dock it would be the Finder. This is the gateway to all of the elements of your computer. It is possible to get to selected items through other routes, but the Finder is the only location where you can gain access to everything on your system. If you ever feel that you are getting lost within OS X, click on the Finder and then you should begin to feel more at home. To access the Finder:

Click once on this icon on the Dock

Overview

The Finder has its own toolbar, a Sidebar from which items can be accessed and a main window where the contents of selected items can be viewed:

Forward and back   View options   Actions button   Search

View all files

Folders are displayed here

Sidebar

Main windows

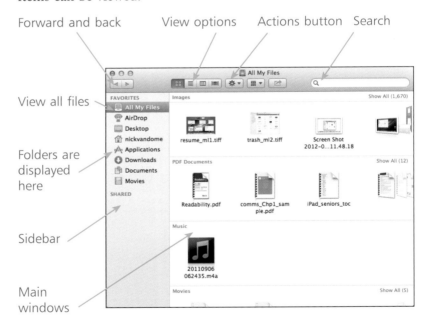

Don't forget

The Actions button has options for displaying information about a selected item and also options for how it is displayed with the Finder.

Finder Folders

All My Files

This contains all of the latest files on which you have been working. They are sorted into categories according to file type so that you can search through them quickly. This is an excellent way to locate items without having to look through lots of folders. To access this:

1 Click on this link in the Finder Sidebar to access the contents of your All My Files folder

2 All of your files are displayed in individual categories. Click on the headings at the top of each category to sort items by criteria

Don't forget

The Finder is always open (as denoted by the graphic underneath its icon on the Dock) and it cannot readily be closed down or removed.

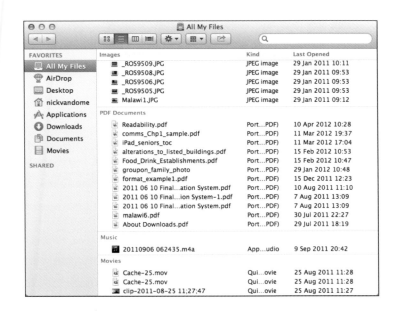

Home folder

This contains the contents of your own home directory, containing your personal folders and files. OS X inserts some pre-named folders which it thinks will be useful, but it is possible to rename, rearrange or delete these as you please. It is also possible to add as many more folders as you want.

1 Click on this link to access the contents of your Home folder

2 The Home folder contains the Public folder that can be used to share files with other users if the computer is part of a network

Applications

This folder contains all of the applications on your iMac. They can also be accessed from the Launchpad as shown in Chapter Seven.

Downloads

This is the default folder for any files or apps that you download (other than those from the Apple App Store).

Documents

This is part of your home folder but is put on the Finder Sidebar for ease of access. New folders can be created for different types of documents.

Hot tip

When you are creating documents OS X, by default, recognizes their type and then, when you save them, suggests the most applicable folder in your Home directory in which to save them. So, if you have created a word processed document, OS X will suggest you save it in Documents; if it is a photograph it will suggest Pictures; if it is a video it will suggest Movies, and so on.

Finder Views

The way in which items are displayed within the Finder can be amended in a variety of ways, depending on how you want to view the contents of a folder. Different folders can have their own viewing options applied to them and these will stay in place until a new option is specified.

Back button

When working within the Finder each new window replaces the previous one, unless you open a new app. This prevents the screen becoming cluttered with dozens of open windows, as you look through various Finder windows for a particular item. To ensure that you never feel lost within the Finder structure, there is a Back button on the Finder toolbar that enables you to retrace the steps that you have taken.

Beware

If you have not opened any Finder windows, the Back button will not operate at all.

1   Navigate to a folder within the Finder (in this case the "Bulgaria" folder contained within Pictures)

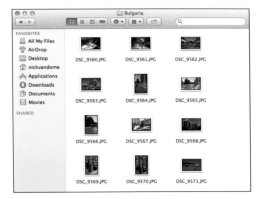

Hot tip

Select an item within the Finder window and click on the space bar to view its details.

2   Click on the Back button to move back to the previously-visited window (in this case, the main Pictures window)

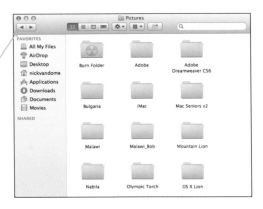

...cont'd

Icon view

One of the viewing options for displaying items within the Finder is as icons. This provides a graphical representation of the items in the Finder. It is possible to customize the way that Icon view looks and functions:

 Click here on the Finder toolbar to access Icon view

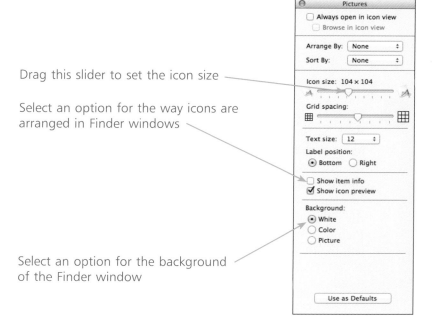 Select View from the Menu bar, check on as Icons and select Show View Options to access the options for customizing Icon view

Drag this slider to set the icon size

Select an option for the way icons are arranged in Finder windows

Select an option for the background of the Finder window

List view

List view can be used to show the items within a Finder window as a list, with additional information shown next to them. This can be a more efficient method than Icon view if there are a lot of items within a folder. List view enables you to see more items at one time and also view the additional information.

1 Click here on the Finder toolbar to access List view

2 The name of each folder or file is displayed here. If any item has additional elements within it, this is represented by a small triangle next to them. Additional information in List view, such as file size and last modified date, is included in columns to the right

Don't forget

List view can be customized to include a variety of information such as file size and date last modified.

Column view

Column view is a useful option if you want to trace the location of a particular item, i.e. see the full path of its location, starting from the hard drive.

1 Click here on the Finder toolbar to access Column view

2 Click on an item to see everything within that folder. If an arrow follows an item it means that there are further items to view

Covers

Covers is another innovative feature on the iMac, that enables you to view items as large icons. This is particularly useful for image files as it enables you to quickly see the details of the image to see if it is the one you want. To use Covers:

1 Select a folder and at the top of the Finder window click on this button

2 The items within the folder are displayed in their cover state

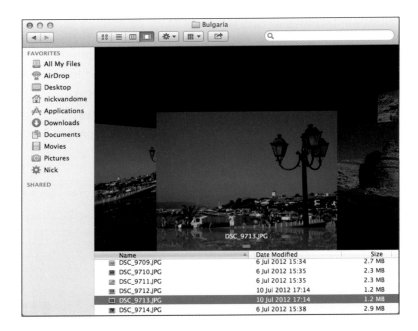

3 Drag with the mouse on each item to view the next one, or click on the slider at the bottom of the window. You can also move between items by swiping left or right on a Trackpad or Magic Mouse

Quick Look

Through a Finder option called Quick Look, it is possible to view the content of a file without having to first open it. To do this:

1 Select a file within the Finder

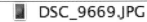

2 Press the space bar

3 The contents of the file are displayed without it opening in its default app

In Quick Look it is even possible to preview videos or presentations without having to first open them in their default app.

Hot tip

4 Click on the cross to close Quick Look

Finder Toolbar

Customizing the toolbar

As with most elements of OS X, it is possible to customize the Finder toolbar:

1 Select View>Customize Toolbar from the Menu bar

2 Drag items from the window into the toolbar, or:

3 Drag the default set of icons into the toolbar

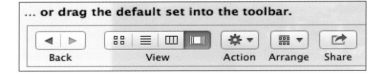

4 Click Done at the bottom of the window

Finder Sidebar

Using the Sidebar

The Sidebar is the left-hand panel of the Finder which can be used to access items on your iMac:

1 Click on a button on the Sidebar

2 Its contents are displayed in the main Finder window

Don't forget

When you click on an item in the Sidebar, its contents are shown in the main Finder window to its right.

Adding to the Sidebar

Items that you access most frequently can be added to the Sidebar. To do this:

Don't forget

When items are added to the Finder Sidebar a shortcut, or alias, is inserted into the Sidebar, not the actual item.

1 Drag an item from the main Finder window onto the Sidebar

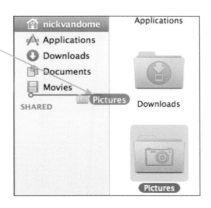

2 The item is added to the Sidebar. You can do this with apps, folders and files

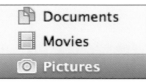

Don't forget

Items can be removed from the Sidebar by Ctrl+clicking on them and selecting Remove from Sidebar from the contextual menu.

Finder Search

Searching electronic data is now a massive industry, with companies such as Google leading the way with online searching. On iMacs it is also possible to search your folders and files, using the built-in search facilities. This can be done either through the Finder or with the Spotlight app.

Using Finder
To search for items within the Finder:

1 In the Finder window, enter the search keyword(s) in this box. Search options are listed below the keyword

2 Select an option for your search

3 In the Search box click on the token next to the keyword. This gives you additional options for what to search over

4 The search results are shown in the Finder window

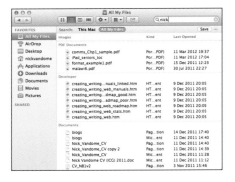

5 Double-click on a file to open it

Copying and Moving items

Items can be copied and moved within OS X by using the copy and paste method or by dragging:

Copy and paste

1 Select an item and select Edit>Copy from the Menu bar

Don't forget

When an item is copied, it is placed on the Clipboard and remains there until another item is copied.

2 Move to the target location and select Edit>Paste Item from the Menu bar. The item is then pasted into the new location

Dragging
Drag a file from one location into another to move it to that location

Hot tip

Hold down the Option key while dragging to copy an item rather than moving it.

Working with Folders

When OS X is installed, there are various folders that have already been created to hold apps and files. Some of these are essential (i.e. those containing apps) while others are created as an aid for where you might want to store the files that you create (such as the Pictures and Movies folders). Once you start working with OS X you will probably want to create your own folders, in which to store and organize your documents. This can be done on the desktop or within any level of your existing folder structure. To create a new folder:

1 Access the location in which you want to create the new folder (e.g. your Home folder) and select File>New Folder from the Menu bar

2 A new, empty, folder is inserted at the selected location (named "untitled folder")

3 Overtype the file name with a new one. Press Enter

4 Double-click on a folder to view its contents (at this point it should be empty)

Spring-loaded Folders

Another method for moving items with the Finder is to use the spring-loaded folder option. This enables you to drag items into a folder and then view the contents of the folder before you drop the item into it. This means that you can drag items into nested folders in a single operation. To do this:

1 Select the item you want to move

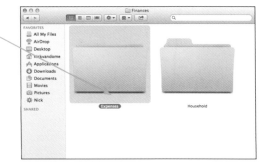

2 Drag the selected item over the folder into which you want to place it. Keep the mouse held down

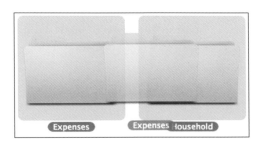

3 The folder will open, revealing its contents. The selected item can either be dropped into the folder or, if there are sub-folders, the same operation can be repeated until you find the folder into which you want to place the selected item

Hot tip

The spring-loaded folder technique can be used to move items between different locations within the Finder, e.g. for moving files from your Pictures folder into your Home folder.

Beware

Do not release the mouse button until you have reached the location into which you want to place the selected item.

Smart Folders

When working on any computer it is inevitable that you will soon have a number of related files in different locations. This could be because you save your images in one folder, your word processing documents in another, web pages in another and so on. This can cause difficulties when you are trying to keep track of a lot of related documents. OS X overcomes this problem through the use of Smart Folders. These are folders that you set up using Finder search results as the foundation. Then when new items are created that meet the original criteria they are automatically included within the Smart Folder. To create a Smart Folder:

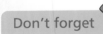
1 Conduct a search with the Finder search box

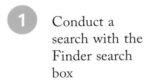

2 Once the search is completed, click the Save button to create a Smart Folder

Save

3 Enter a name for the new Smart Folder and click Save

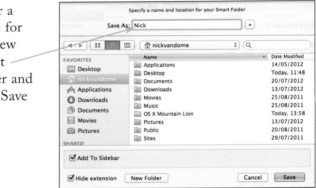

4 The Smart Folder is added to the Finder Sidebar. Click the Smart Folder to view its contents

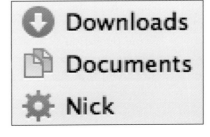

Selecting Items

Apps and files within OS X folders can be selected by a variety of different methods:

Selecting by dragging

Drag the cursor to encompass the items to be selected. The selected items will become highlighted.

Selecting by clicking

Click once on an item to select it, hold down Shift and then click on another item in a list to select a consecutive group of items.

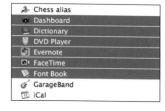

To select a non-consecutive group, select the first item by clicking on it once, then hold down the Command key (the one with the Apple symbol on it) and select the other required items. The selected items will appear highlighted.

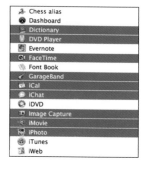

Select All

To select all of the items in a folder, select Edit>Select All from the Menu bar:

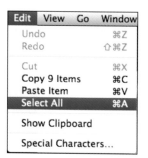

Don't forget

Once items have been selected, a single command can be applied to all of them. For instance, you can copy a group of items by selecting them and then applying the Copy command from the Menu bar.

Don't forget

The Select All command selects all of the elements within the active item. For instance, if the active item is a word processing document, the Select All command will select all of the items within the document; if it is a folder it will select all of the items within that folder.

Actions Button

The Finder Actions button provides a variety of options for any item, or items, selected in the Finder. To use this:

1 Select an item, or group of items, about which you want to find out additional information

Bulgaria18.JPG

2 Click on the Actions button on the Finder toolbar

3 The available options for the selected item, or items, are displayed. These include Get Info, which displays additional information about an item, such as file type, file size, creation and modification dates and the default app for opening the item

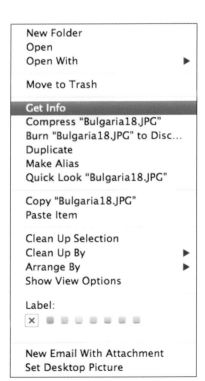

New Folder
Open
Open With ▶

Move to Trash

Get Info
Compress "Bulgaria18.JPG"
Burn "Bulgaria18.JPG" to Disc...
Duplicate
Make Alias
Quick Look "Bulgaria18.JPG"

Copy "Bulgaria18.JPG"
Paste Item

Clean Up Selection
Clean Up By ▶
Arrange By ▶
Show View Options

Label:
×

New Email With Attachment
Set Desktop Picture

Sharing from the Finder

Next but one to the Actions button on the Finder is the Share button. This can be used to share a selected item, or items, in a variety of ways appropriate to the type of file that has been selected. For instance, a photo will have options including the photo-sharing site Flickr while a text document will have fewer options. To share items directly from the Finder:

Hot tip

The Share button is available from many apps throughout Mountain Lion. This means that there is increased functionality for sharing items. For instance, you can share Web pages from Safari or share photos from iPhoto. In the autumn/ fall of 2012 this share facility will extend to Facebook.

1. Locate and select the item(s) that you want to share

2. Click on the Share button on the Finder toolbar and select one of the options

Don't forget

In between the Actions and the Share buttons on the Finder is a button for changing the arrangement of items within the Finder. Click on this button to access arrangement options such as Name, Kind, Date and Size.

3. For some of the options, such as Twitter and Flickr, you will be asked to add an account. If you already have an account with these services you can enter the details or, if not, you can create a new account

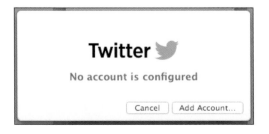

Menus

The main Apple Menu bar in OS X contains a variety of menus, which are consistent regardless of the app in operation:

- **Apple menu**. This is denoted by a translucent blue apple and contains general information about the computer, a preferences option for changing the functionality and appearance of the Dock and options for closing down the computer

- **Finder menu**. This contains preferences options for amending the functionality and appearance of the Finder and also options for emptying the Trash and accessing other apps (under the Services option)

- **File menu**. This contains common commands for working with open documents, such as opening and closing files, creating aliases, moving to the Trash, ejecting external devices and burning discs

- **Edit menu**. This contains common commands that apply to the majority of apps used on the iMac. These include Undo, Cut, Copy, Paste, Select All and show the contents of the clipboard, i.e. items that have been cut or copied

- **View**. This contains options for how windows and folders are displayed within the Finder and for customizing the Finder toolbar

- **Go**. This can be used to navigate around your computer. This includes moving to your Home folder, your Applications folder, recently-opened items and also remote servers for connecting to other computers on a network

- **Window**. This contains commands to organize the currently-open apps and files on your desktop

- **Help**. This contains the Mac Help files which contain information about all aspects of OS X Mountain Lion

6 Navigating in Mountain Lion

OS X Mountain Lion introduces Multi-Touch Gestures for navigating around your apps and documents. This chapter looks at how to use this to get around your iMac.

A New Way of Navigating

One of the most revolutionary features of OS X Mountain Lion is the way in which you can navigate around your applications, web pages and documents. This involves a much greater reliance on swiping on a Trackpad or adapted mouse; techniques that have been imported from the iPhone and the iPad. These are known as Multi-Touch Gestures and work with two devices on the iMac:

- **A Magic Mouse**. This is an external mouse that works wirelessly via Bluetooth

- **A Magic Trackpad**. This is an external trackpad that works wirelessly via Bluetooth

These devices work using a swiping technique with fingers moving over their surface. This should be done with a light touch; it is a gentle swipe, rather than any pressure being applied to the device.

The Magic Mouse and Magic Keypad do not have any buttons in the same way as traditional devices. Instead, specific areas are clickable so that you can still perform left- and right-click operations. On a Magic Mouse the center and right side can be used for clicking operations and on a Magic Trackpad the left and right corners can perform the same tasks:

No More Scroll Bars

Another innovation in OS X Mountain Lion is the removal of scroll bars that are constantly visible on a web page or document. Instead, there are scroll bars that only appear when you are moving around a page or document. When you stop, the scroll bars melt away. Scrolling is done by Multi-Touch Gestures on a Magic Trackpad or Magic Mouse and these gestures are looked at on the following pages. To perform scrolling with OS X Mountain Lion:

Don't forget

Web pages and document windows can also be navigated around by dragging on the scroll bars using a mouse or a trackpad.

1 Scroll around a web page or document by swiping up or down on a Magic Mouse or a Magic Trackpad. As you move up or down a page the scroll bar appears

Hot tip

The way scroll bars operate on your iMac can be set within the General option within the System Preferences.

89

2 When you stop scrolling the bar disappears, to allow optimum viewing area for your web page or document

Magic Trackpad Gestures

Pointing and clicking

A Magic Trackpad can be used to perform a variety of pointing and clicking tasks.

1 Tap with one finger in the middle of the Magic Trackpad to perform a single click operation, e.g. to click on a button or click on an open window

2 Tap once with two fingers in the middle of the Magic Trackpad to access any contextual menus associated with an item (this is the equivalent of the traditional right-click with a mouse)

3 Highlight a word or phrase and double-tap with three fingers to see look-up information for the selected item. This is frequently a dictionary definition but it can also be a Wikipedia entry

4 Move over an item and drag with three fingers to move the item around the screen

Beware

If you have too many functions set using the same number of fingers, some of them may not work. See page 101 for details about setting preferences for Multi-Touch Gestures.

...cont'd

Scrolling and zooming

One of the most common operations on a computer is scrolling on a page, whether it is a web page or a document. Traditionally, this has been done with a mouse and a cursor. However, using a Magic Trackpad you can now do all of your scrolling with your fingers. There are a number of options for doing this:

Scrolling up and down

To move up and down web pages or documents, use two fingers on the Magic Trackpad and swipe up or down. The page moves in the opposite direction to the one in which you are swiping, i.e. if you swipe up, the page moves down and vice versa:

Don't forget

Don't worry if you cannot immediately get the hang of Multi-Touch Gestures. It takes a bit of practice to get the correct touch and pressure on the Magic Trackpad, or the Magic Mouse.

1 Open a web page

2 Position two fingers in the middle of the Magic Trackpad

3 Swipe them up to move down the page

Don't forget

When scrolling up and down pages, the gesture moves the page the opposite way, i.e. swipe down to move up the page and vice versa.

4 Swipe them down to move up a page

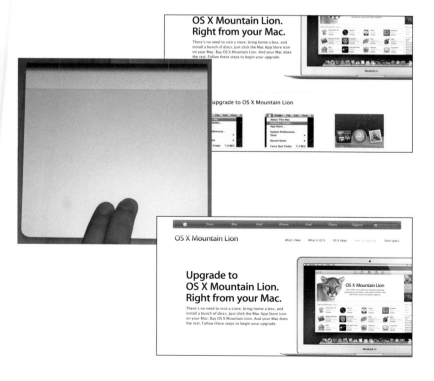

...cont'd

Zooming in and out

To zoom in or out on web pages or documents:

1 To zoom in, position your thumb and forefinger in the middle of the Magic Trackpad

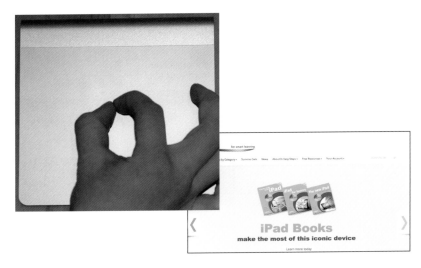

2 Spread them outwards to zoom in on a web page or document

3 To zoom out, position your thumb and forefinger at opposite corners of the Magic Trackpad

Don't forget

There is a limit on how far you can zoom in or out on a web page or document, to ensure that it does not distort the content too much.

4 Swipe them into the center of the Magic Trackpad to zoom out

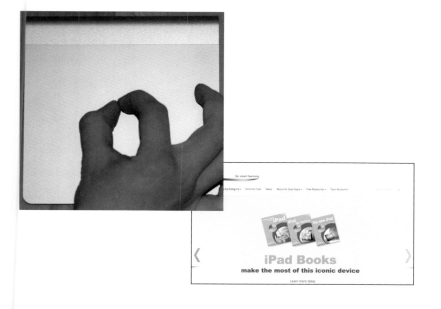

...cont'd

Moving between pages

With Multi-Touch Gestures it is possible to swipe between pages within a document. To do this:

1 Position two fingers to the left or right of the Magic Trackpad

2 Swipe to the opposite side of the Magic Trackpad to move through the document

Moving between full-screen apps

In addition to moving between pages by swiping, it is also possible to move between different apps, when they are in full-screen mode. To do this:

Don't forget

See Chapter Seven for details about using full-screen apps.

1 Position three fingers to the left or right of the Magic Trackpad

2 Swipe to the opposite side of the Magic Trackpad to move through the available full-screen apps

Showing the Desktop

To show the whole Desktop, regardless of how many files or apps are open:

1   Position your thumb and three fingers in the middle of the Magic Trackpad

2   Swipe to the opposite corners of the Magic Trackpad to display the Desktop

3   The Desktop is displayed, with all items minimized around the side of the screen

Magic Mouse Gestures

Pointing and clicking

A Magic Mouse can be used to perform a variety of pointing and clicking tasks.

1 Click with one finger on the Magic Mouse to perform a single-click operation, e.g. to select a button or command

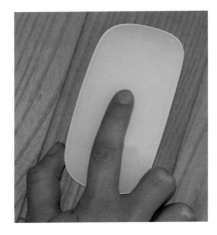

2 Tap with one finger on the right side of the Magic Mouse to access any contextual menus associated with an item (this is the equivalent of the traditional right-click with a mouse)

Don't forget

The right-click operation can be set within the Mouse System Preferences.

Scrolling and zooming

The Magic Mouse can also be used to perform scrolling and zooming functions within a web page or document

1 Swipe up or down with one finger to move up and down a web page or document

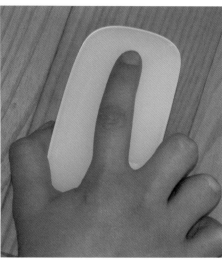

Don't forget

When scrolling on a web page or document, it moves in the opposite direction to the movement of your finger, i.e. if you swipe up, the page moves down and vice versa.

2 Double-tap with one finger to zoom in on a web page

...cont'd

3 Swipe left or right with one finger to move between pages

4 Swipe left or right with two fingers to move between full-screen apps

Multi-Touch Preferences

Some Multi-Touch Gestures only have a single action, which cannot be changed. However, others have options for changing the action for a specific gesture. This is done within the respective preferences for the Magic Mouse or the Magic Trackpad, where a full list of Multi-Touch Gestures is shown. To use these:

1 Access the System Preferences and click on the Mouse or Trackpad button

Mouse

2 Click on one of the tabs at the top

More Gestures

3 The actions are described on the left, with a graphic explanation on the right

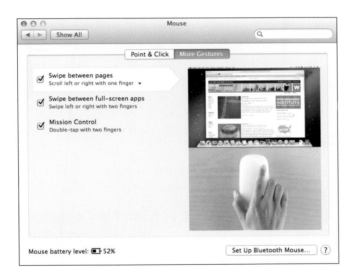

Don't forget

The Magic Trackpad has three tabbed options within the System Preferences: Point & Click, Scroll & Zoom and More Gestures. The Magic Mouse has preferences for Point & Click and More Gestures.

101

4 If there is a down arrow next to an option, click on it to change the way an action is activated

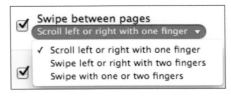

...cont'd

Trackpad Gestures

The full list of Magic Trackpad Multi-Touch Gestures, with their default action are: (relevant ones for Magic Mouse are in brackets)

Point & Click

- Tap to click – tap once with one finger (same for the Magic Mouse)

- Secondary click – click or tap with two fingers (single-click on the right of the Magic Mouse)

- Look up – double-tap with three fingers

- Three finger drag – move with three fingers

Scroll & Zoom

- Scroll direction: natural – content tracks finger movement, with two fingers (one finger with the Magic Mouse)

- Zoom in or out – pinch or spread with two fingers

- Smart zoom – double-tap with two fingers (double-tap with one finger with the Magic Mouse)

- Rotate – rotate with two fingers

More Gestures

- Swipe between pages – scroll left or right with two fingers (scroll left or right with one finger with the Magic Mouse)

- Swipe between full-screen apps – swipe left or right with three fingers (swipe left or right with two fingers with the Magic Mouse)

- To access the Notification Center – swipe left from the right-hand edge of a Trackpad or Magic Trackpad

- Access Mission Control – swipe up with three fingers (double-tap with two fingers with the Magic Mouse)

- App Exposé – swipe down with three fingers

- Access Launchpad – pinch with thumb and three fingers

- Show Desktop – spread with thumb and three fingers

Mission Control

Mission Control is a function in OS X Mountain Lion that helps you organize all of your open apps, full-screen apps and documents. It also enables you to quickly view the Dashboard and Desktop. Within Mission Control there are also Spaces, where you can group together similar types of documents. To use Mission Control:

1 Click on this button on the Dock, or

Don't forget

Click on a window in Mission Control to access it and exit the Mission Control window.

2 Swipe upwards with three fingers on the Trackpad or double-tap with two fingers on a Magic Mouse

 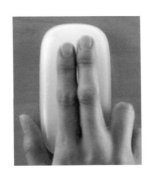

3 All open files and apps are visible via Mission Control

Don't forget

The top row of Mission Control contains the Dashboard, the Desktop and any full-screen apps.

...cont'd

4 If there is more than one window open for an app they will be grouped together by Mission Control

5 If an app is made full-screen it automatically appears along the top row

6 Desktop items are grouped together on the top row within Mission Control within an area called a Space (see next two pages)

Spaces and Exposé

The top level of Mission Control contains Spaces, which are areas into which you can group certain apps, e.g. the iLife apps such as iPhoto and iTunes. This means that you can access these apps independently from every other open item. This helps organize your apps and files. To use Spaces:

1 Move the cursor over the top right-hand corner of Mission Control

Don't forget

Preferences for Spaces and Exposé can be set within the Mission Control System Preference.

2 A new Space is created along the top row of Mission Control

Desktop 2

Hot tip

Create different Spaces for different types of content, e.g. one for productivity and one for entertainment.

3 Drag an app onto the Space

Desktop 2

4 Drag additional apps onto the Space

Desktop 2

...cont'd

5 When you create additional Spaces the content of each is shown on its own when you access Mission Control

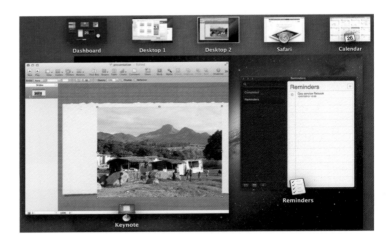

Don't forget

When you create a new space it can subsequently be deleted by moving the cursor over it and clicking on the cross at the left-hand corner. Any items that have been added to a Space that is then deleted are returned to the default Desktop Space.

Exposé

Exposé is a function that enables you to view all of the open documents within an app. To use this:

1 Position three fingers at the top of the Magic Trackpad and swipe down

2 The open documents for the current app are displayed

Hot tip

If you are using a Magic Mouse, the Exposé function can be set with the F keys in the Mission Control System Preference. This is done within the Applications Windows option.

7 iMac Apps

Apps, or applications, are the programs with which you start putting Mountain Lion to use, either for work or for fun. This chapter looks at accessing your apps and obtaining more via the online Mac App Store.

Launchpad

Even though the Dock can be used to store shortcuts to your applications, it is limited in terms of space. The full set of applications on your iMac can be found in the Finder (see Chapter Five) but OS X Mountain Lion has a feature that allows you to quickly access and manage all of your applications. These include the ones that are pre-installed on your iMac and also any that you install yourself or download from the Apple App Store. This feature is called Launchpad. To use it:

1 Click once on this button on the Dock

Hot tip

If the apps take up more than one screen, swipe from right to left with two fingers to view the additional pages. (For more information on Multi-Touch Gestures, see Chapter Six.)

2 All of the apps are displayed

Don't forget

To launch an app from within Launchpad, click on it once.

3 Similar types of apps can be grouped together in individual folders. By default, the Utilities are grouped in this way

4 To create a group of similar apps, drag the icon for one over another

5 The apps are grouped together in a folder and Launchpad gives it a name, based on the types of apps within the folder

6 To change the name, click on it once and overtype it with the new name

7 The folder appears within the Launchpad window

8 To remove an app, click and hold on it until it starts to jiggle and a cross appears. Click on the cross to remove it

Don't forget

System apps, i.e. the ones that already come with your iMac, cannot be removed in the Launchpad, only ones that you have downloaded.

Full-Screen Apps

When working with apps we all like to be able to see as much of a window as possible. With OS X Mountain Lion this is possible with the full-screen app. This allows you to expand an app with this functionality so that it takes up the whole of your monitor or screen with a minimum of toolbars visible. Some apps have this functionality but some do not. To use full-screen apps:

1 By default an app appears on the desktop with other windows behind it

Don't forget

If the button in Step 2 is not visible then the app does not have the full-screen functionality.

2 Click on this button at the top right-hand corner of the app's window

3 The app is expanded to take up the whole window. The main Apple Menu bar and the Dock are hidden

4 To view the main Menu bar, move the cursor over the top of the screen

5 You can move between all full-screen apps by swiping with three fingers left or right on a Trackpad or Magic Mouse

 Hot tip

For more information about navigating with Multi-Touch Gestures see Chapter Six.

6 Move the cursor over the top right-hand corner of the screen and click on this button to close the full-screen functionality

7 In Mission Control all of the open full-screen apps are shown in the top row

OS X Apps

OS X Mountain Lion apps include:

- **Automator**. An app for creating automated processes

- **Calculator.** A basic calculator

- **Calendar**. The Mountain Lion calendar app

- **Chess**. Play online chess against your iMac

- **Contacts**. An app for storing contact information

- **Dashboard**. A set of useful widgets, accessed from the Dock or the F12 key

- **Dictionary**. A digital dictionary

- **DVD Player.** Plays and views DVDs

- **FaceTime.** Can be used for video calls (See Chapter Eight)

- **Font Book.** Use this to add and change fonts

- **Front Row**. An app for accessing music, movies or photos with a remote control

- **Image Capture**. For downloading digital images

- **iPhoto, iTunes, iMovie, iDVD and GarageBand.** (See Chapter Nine)

- **Mail**. The default email app

- **Mission Control.** The function for organizing your desktop

- **Notes**. An app for creating and sharing notes

- **Photo Booth.** An app for creating photo effects

- **Preview.** Can be used to view a variety of different file types

- **QuickTime Player**. The default application for viewing video

- **Reminders**. App for setting reminders

- **Safari**. The OS X specific web browser

- **TextEdit**. An app for editing text files

- **Time Machine**. OS X's backup facility

Accessing the App Store

The App Store is another OS X app. This is an online facility where you can download and buy new apps. These cover a range of categories such as productivity, business and entertainment. When you select or buy an app from the App Store, it is downloaded automatically by Launchpad and appears here next to the rest of the apps.

To buy apps from the App Store you need to have an Apple ID and account. If you have not already set this up, it can be done when you first access the App Store. To use the App Store:

Don't forget

The App Store is an online function so you will need an Internet connection to access it.

1 Click on this icon on the Dock or within the Launchpad

2 The homepage of the App Store contains the current top-featured apps

Hot tip

You can set up an Apple ID when you first set up your iMac or you can do it when you register for the App Store or the iTunes Store.

3 Your account information and Quick Link categories are listed at the right-hand side of the page

Downloading Apps

The App Store contains a wide range of apps: from small, fun apps, to powerful productivity ones. However, downloading them from the App Store is the same regardless of the type of app. The only differences are whether they require payment or not and the length of time they take to download. To download an app from the App Store:

1 Browse through the App Store until you find the required app

2 Click on the app to view a detailed description about it

3 Click on the button underneath the app icon to download it. If there is no charge for the app the button will say Free

4 If there is a charge for the app, the button will say Buy App

5 Click on the Install App button

6 Enter your Apple ID account details to continue downloading the app

Sign in to download from the App Store.
If you have an Apple ID, sign in with it here. If you have used the iTunes Store or MobileMe, for example, you have an Apple ID. If you don't have an Apple ID, click Create Apple ID.

Apple ID
nickvandome@mac.com

Password   Forgot?

Create Apple ID   Cancel   Sign In

7 The progress of the download is displayed in a progress bar underneath the Launchpad icon on the Dock

Don't forget

Depending on their size, different apps take differing amounts of time to be downloaded.

8 Once it has been downloaded, the app is available within Launchpad

TextEdit   Time Machine

Pages   SoundCloud

Don't forget

As you download more apps, additional pages will be created within the Launchpad to accommodate them.

115

Finding Apps

There are thousands of apps in the App Store and sometimes the hardest task is locating the ones you want. However, there are a number of ways in which finding apps is made as easy as possible.

1 Click on the Featured button

2 The main window has a range of categories such as New, What's Hot and Staff Favorites. At the right-hand side there is a panel with the Top Ten Paid For apps

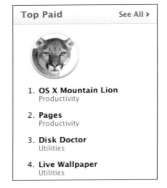

3 Underneath this is a list of the Top Ten Free apps

4 Click on the Top Charts button to display top apps for different categories

5 Click on the Categories button to browse through the apps by specific categories, such as Business, Entertainment and Finance

Managing Your Apps

Once you have bought apps from the App Store you can view details of ones you have purchased and also install updated versions of them.

Purchased Apps
To view your purchased apps:

1 Click on the Purchased button

2 Details of your purchased apps are displayed (including those that are free)

Don't forget

Even if you interrupt a download and turn off your iMac you will still be able to resume the download when you restart your computer.

3 If a download of an app has been interrupted, click on the Resume button to continue with it

Paused	RESUME
2.85 MB of 242.32 MB	

Updating Apps
Improvements and fixes are being developed constantly and these can be downloaded to ensure that all of your apps are up to date.

Hot tip

It is always worth updating your apps to improve them and download any security fixes as required.

1 When updates are available this is indicated by a red circle on the App Store icon in the Dock

2 Click on the Updates button

3 Click on the Update button to update an individual app

117

Sharing Apps

If you have more than one Mac computer you do not have to buy apps separately for each one. If you have purchased an app for one iMac you can also install it on other Macs without having to pay for it again. To do this:

1 Access the App Store and click on the Purchased button

2 Any apps that have been purchased on another Mac are displayed in the Purchased window

Purchases		Purchase Date
Keynote Apple®		17 August 2011
SoundCloud SoundCloud Ltd.		17 August 2011
Plane Control Lite Istom Games Kft.		03 August 2011
Full Deck Solitaire GRL Games		03 August 2011
Pages Apple®		31 July 2011
Evernote Evernote		30 July 2011

3 Click on the Install button to install an app on a Mac that does not yet have it

4 To install the app you will need to enter your Apple ID, although you will not be charged for the app

8 Internet and Email

This chapter shows how to get the most out of the Internet and email. It covers connecting to the Internet and how to use the OS X web browser, Safari, and its email app, Mail. It also covers Messages for text and photo messaging and FaceTime for video messaging and chatting.

Getting Connected

Access to the Internet is an accepted part of the computing world and it is unusual for users not to want to do this. Not only does this provide a gateway to the World Wide Web but also email.

Connecting to the Internet with an iMac is done through the System Preferences. To do this:

Don't forget

Before you connect to the Internet you have to have an Internet Service Provider (ISP) who will provide you with the relevant method of connection, i.e. dial-up, cable or broadband. They will provide you with any login details.

1 Click on the System Preferences icon on the Dock

2 Click on the Network icon

3 Check that your method of connecting to the Internet is active, i.e. colored green

4 Click on the Assist me... button to access wizards for connecting to the Internet with your preferred method of connection

5 Click on the Assistant... button

6 The Network Setup Assistant is used to configure your system so that you can connect to the Internet

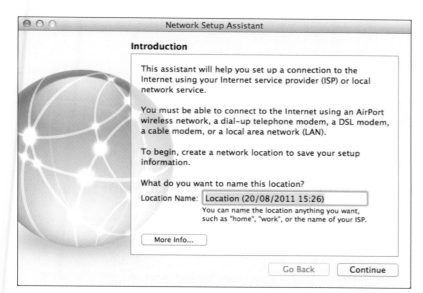

Network Setup Assistant

Introduction

This assistant will help you set up a connection to the Internet using your Internet service provider (ISP) or local network service.

You must be able to connect to the Internet using an AirPort wireless network, a dial-up telephone modem, a DSL modem, a cable modem, or a local area network (LAN).

To begin, create a network location to save your setup information.

What do you want to name this location?

Location Name: Location (20/08/2011 15:26)

You can name the location anything you want, such as "home", "work", or the name of your ISP.

More Info...

Go Back   Continue

Don't forget

In a lot of cases your iMac will recognize your Wi-Fi connection, if you have one, and connect to the Internet automaticallly.

121

7 Enter a name for your connection

Location Name: My home

8 Click on the Continue button

Continue

...cont'd

9 Select an option for how you will connect to the Internet, e.g. wireless, cable or telephone modem

10 Click on the Continue button

11 For a wireless connection, select an available wireless network. This will be the router that is being used to make the connection

Select the wireless network you want to join:

CRAIGIE1

juicyanno

NETGEAR

12 Enter a password for the router (this will have been created when you connected and configured the router)

Password: Selected network requires a password

••••••••

13 Click on the Continue button   Continue

14 The Ready to Connect window informs you that you are about to attempt to connect to your network

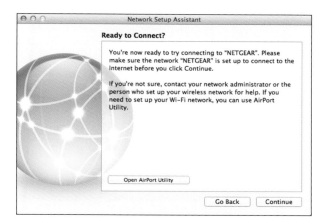

15 Click on the Continue button

16 You are informed if the connection has been successful

17 Click on the Done button

Safari

Safari is a web browser that is designed specifically to be used with OS X. It is similar in most respects to other browsers, but it usually functions more quickly and works seamlessly with OS X.

Safari overview

1 Click here on the Dock to launch Safari

2 All of the controls are at the top of the browser

Toolbar   Address/Search bar   Reader Tabs

Bookmarks
Bar and
buttons

Smart Search box

One of the innovations in the latest version (at the time of printing) of Safari (6) is that the Address bar and the Search box have been incorporated into one item. You can use the same box for searching for an item or enter a Web address to go to that page.

1 Click in the box to enter an item

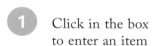

2 Results are presented as web pages or search results. Click on the appropriate one to go to that item, i.e. directly to a website or to the search results page

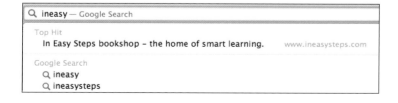

Sharing pages

As with many features in Mountain Lion, web pages can be shared directly from Safari. To do this, first open a web page.

1 Click on this button and select one of the sharing options

Using iCloud

Safari also makes use of the power of iCloud; if you are browsing the web on another iCloud-enabled device, the tabs that you have open are available on the computer you are using with Mountain Lion.

1 Click on this button

2 Open pages on other devices are shown. Click on one of these to open it

Preferences

Select Safari>Preferences from the Menu bar to specify settings for the way Safari operates and displays web pages.

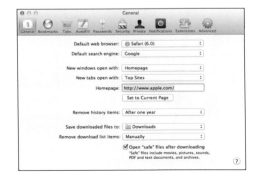

> ### Hot tip
>
> In the Preferences window, click on the Passwords button to view the passwords that you have used on specific websites.

Safari Tabbed Browsing

Tabs are now a familiar feature on web browsers, so you can have multiple sites open within the same browser window.

1 When more than one tab is open, the tabs appear at the top of the web pages

| Apple | In Easy Steps bookshop – the home of sm... | ✢ | ▭ |

2 Click on this button next to the tabs to open a new tab

3 Click on one of the Top Sites (see page 127) or enter a website address in the Address bar

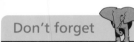

Don't forget

Safari is a full-screen app and can be expanded by clicking the double arrow in the top-right corner. For more information on Full-Screen Apps, see Chapter Seven.

4 Click on this button next to the New Tab button to minimize all of the current tabs

5 Move left and right to view all of the open tabs in thumbnail view. Click on one to view it at full size

Safari Top Sites

Within Safari there is a facility to view a graphical representation of the websites that you visit most frequently. This can be done from a button on the Safari Menu bar. To do this:

1 Click on this button to view the Top Sites window

2 The Top Sites window contains thumbnails of the websites that you have visited most frequently with Safari (this builds up as you visit more sites)

3 Click on the Edit button to change the properties of the Top Sites thumbnails

4 Click on the cross to delete a thumbnail from the Top Sites window. Click on the pin to keep it there permanently

5 Click on a thumbnail to go to the full site

6 Use these buttons to select the size of the thumbnails

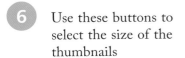

7 To add a new site to the Top Sites, open another window and drag the URL (website address) into the Top Sites

Don't forget

The Top Sites window is also accessed if you open a new tab within Safari.

Safari Reader

Web pages can be complex and cluttered at times. On occasions you may want to just read the content of one story on a web page without all of the extra material in view. In Safari this can be done with the Reader function. To do this:

1 Select View>Show Reader from the Safari menu bar

2 Click on the Reader button in the address bar of a web page that supports this functionality

3 The button turns a darker blue once the Reader is activated

4 The content is displayed in a text format, with any photos from the original

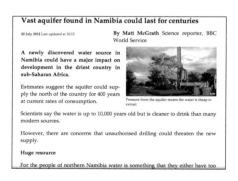

5 Click on this button on the Safari toolbar if you want to save a page to read at a later date

6 Click on this button to add the page to your Reading List

Adding Bookmarks

Bookmarks allow you to create quick links to your favorite web pages or the ones you visit most frequently. Bookmarks can be added to a menu or the Bookmarks Bar in Safari which makes them even quicker to access. Folders can also be created to store the less frequently used bookmarks. To view and create bookmarks:

1 Click here to view all bookmarks

2 All of the saved bookmarks can be accessed from the Collections window and viewed in the main window. Click on a page to move to it

Don't forget

The Bookmarks Bar appears at the top of the browser window.

3 Click here to create a bookmark for the page currently being viewed

Beware

Only keep your most frequently used bookmarks in the Bookmarks Bar. Otherwise some of them will cease to be visible, as there will be too many entries for the available space.

4 Enter a name for the bookmark and select a location in which to store it

5 Click on the Add button

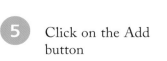

Mail

Email is an essential element for most computer users and iMacs come with their own email app called Mail. This covers all of the email functionality that anyone could need.

When first using Mail you have to set up your email account. This information will be available from the company which provides your email service, although in some cases Mail may obtain this information automatically. To view your Mail account details:

130

1. Click on this icon on the Dock

2. Select Mail>Preferences from the Menu bar

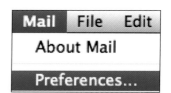

3. Click on the Accounts tab

4. If it has not already been included, enter the details of your email account in the Account Information section

5. Click on this button to add a new email account

Using Email

Mail enables you to send and receive emails and also format them to your own style. This can be simply formatting text or adding customized stationery. To use Mail:

1 Click on the Get Mail button to download available email messages

2 Click on the New Message button to create a new email

3 Enter a recipient in the To: box, a title in the Subject: box and then text for the email in the main window

4 Click on the Format button to access options for formatting the text in the email

5 Click on these buttons to Reply to, Reply to All or Forward an email you have received

6 Select or open an email and click on the Delete button to remove it

Hot tip

To show the text underneath an icon in Mail, Ctrl+click next to an icon and select Icon & Text from the menu.

Hot tip

When entering the name of a recipient for a message, Mail will display details of matching names from your Contacts. For instance, if you type DA, all of the entries in your Contacts beginning with this will be displayed and you can select the required one.

Hot tip

If you Forward an email with an attachment then the attachment is included. If you Reply to an email the attachment will not be included.

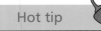

Hot tip

It is worth occasionally checking in your Junk mailbox, in case something you want has been put there.

Beware

Do not send files that are too large in terms of file size, otherwise the recipient may find it takes too long to download.

7 Click on the Junk button to mark an email as junk or spam. This trains Mail to identify junk mail. After a period of time, these types of messages will automatically be moved straight into the Junk mailbox

8 Click on the Attach button to browse your folders to include another file in your email. This can be items such as photos, word documents or PDF files

9 Click on the Photo Browser button to browse photos to add to an email

10 Click on the Show Stationery button to access a variety of templated designs that can be added to your email

11 Select a Stationery design to add it to the email. Elements such as the text and photos can then be edited

Email Conversations

Within Mail you can view conversations, i.e. groups of emails on the same subject. There is also a facility for showing your own replies within a conversation. To view a conversation:

1 Select View>Organize by Conversation from the Mail menu bar

2 Emails with the same subject are grouped together as a conversation in the left-hand pane. The number of grouped emails is shown at the right-hand side

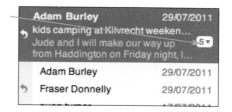

3 Click here to view the full list of emails

4 The full conversation is shown in the right-hand pane

5 Click on this button to include your own messages in a conversation

Show Related Messages

6 Click on this button to hide your own messages in a conversation

Hide Related Messages

Adding Mailboxes

When you are dealing with email it is a good idea to create a folder structure (mailboxes) for your messages. This will allow you to sort your emails into relevant subjects when you receive them, rather than having all of them sitting in your Inbox. To add a structure of new mailboxes

1 Click on this button to view your current mailboxes

2 Click on the plus button at the bottom left-hand corner of the Mail window and select New Mailbox

3 Enter a name for the Mailbox and a location for where you would like it to be stored (by default this will be On My Mac)

4 The new mailbox is added to the current list

Messaging

The Messages app enables you to send text messages (iMessages) to other Mountain Lion users or those with an iPhone, iPad or iPod Touch using iOS 5 or above. It can also be used to send photos, videos and make FaceTime calls. To use Messages:

1 Click on this icon on the Dock

2 Click on this button to start a new conversation

3 Click on this button and select a contact (these will be from your Contacts app). To send an iMessage the recipient has to have an Apple ID

4 The person with whom you are having a conversation is displayed in the left-hand panel

5 The conversation continues down the right-hand panel. Click here to write a message and press Return to send it. Drag photos or videos here to include them too

FaceTime

FaceTime is an app that has previously been used on the iPhone and iPod Touch to make video calls to other compatible devices. However, this is now available with OS X Mountain Lion so that you can make and receive video calls from your iMac via iPhone, iPad and iPod Touches. To do this:

1 Click on this icon on the Dock

2 You require an Apple ID to use FaceTime. Enter your details or click on the Create New Account button

3 Once you have logged in you can make video calls by selecting people from your address book, or adding their phone number, providing they have a device that supports FaceTime

9 Digital Lifestyle

Leisure time, and how we use it, is a significant issue for everyone. Within the OS X environment there are several apps that can be used to create and manage your digital lifestyle. Some of these are known as the iLife suite of apps and cover photos, music, home movies, DVD creation and composing music. Playing games is also covered.

iPhoto

iPhoto is the photo management app for OS X. The intention of iPhoto is to make the organizing, manipulation and sharing of digital images as easy as possible. To begin using iPhoto and downloading photos:

Don't forget

Once a camera has been connected to your iMac, iPhoto should open automatically.

1 Click once on this icon on the Dock

2 Connect your digital camera, or card reader, to your iMac via either USB or Firewire. The images on the connected device are displayed in the main iPhoto window

Don't forget

The iMac has a slot on the side for an SD memory card from which photos can also be downloaded.

3 Click on the Import button to import all of the images from the camera, or card reader

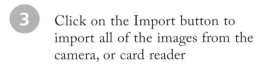
Import 641 Photos

Don't forget

iPhoto is part of the iLife suite of apps that covers items such as photos, music and video.

4 Select specific images and click on the Import Selected button

Import Selected

Once photographs have been downloaded by iPhoto they are displayed within the Library. This is the main storage area for all of the photographs that are added to iPhoto.

Viewing Photos

There are a variety of ways in which photos can be viewed and displayed in iPhoto:

1 In the main window double-click on an image

2 This displays it at full size (click on it once to return to the main window)

Hot tip

Zooming right in on a photo is an excellent way to view fine detail and see if the photo is properly in focus.

3 In the main window drag this slider to display images in the main iPhoto window at different sizes

Organizing Photos

Within iPhoto you can create albums to store different types of photos. To do this:

1 Select photos within the iPhoto window and click on the Add To button at the bottom right-corner of the main window

2 Click on the Album button

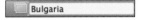

3 Click on the New Album button

4 Enter a name for the Album

5 The new album is included under the Albums section in the left-hand panel

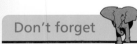

Don't forget

Once photos have been added to an album they are still visible in the main Library. The items in each album are just a reference back to the Library items.

6 To add photos to an album, drag them over the album name from the main iPhoto window

Editing and Sharing Photos

As well as using iPhoto for viewing and organizing photos there are also facilities for editing and sharing them:

1 Click on this button to access the editing options

2 Click on the Quick Fixes tab for options to quickly edit various aspects of a photo, such as rotating it, color editing techniques and cropping

3 Click on the Effects tab to access various special effects that can be applied to a photo

4 Click on the Adjust tab to access a range of more sophisticated color editing options

Beware

Most photos will benefit from some degree of editing but be careful not to overdo it, particularly with color editing and adjustments.

5 Click on the Share button to access options for sharing your photos to photo-sharing sites and also popular social networking sites

iTunes

Music is one of the areas that has revived Apple's fortunes in recent years, primarily through the iPod music player and iTunes, and also the iTunes music store, where music can be bought online. iTunes is a versatile app but its basic function is to play a music CD. To do this:

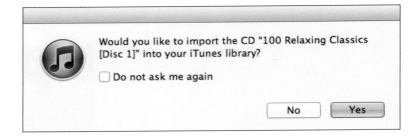

1 Click on this button on the Dock and insert the CD in the CD/DVD drive

2 By default, iTunes will open and display this window. Click No if you just want to play the CD

Would you like to import the CD "100 Relaxing Classics [Disc 1]" into your iTunes library?

☐ Do not ask me again

No   Yes

Beware

Never import music and use it for commercial purposes as this would be a breach of copyright.

3 Click on the CD name

DEVICES

⦿ 100 Relaxing Classics... ⏏

4 Click on this button to play the whole CD

5 Click on the Import CD button if you want to copy (burn) the music from the CD onto your hard drive

Import CD

Managing Your Music

iTunes has a variety of ways to display and manage your music:

 Click on the Music link to see all of the music items within iTunes

 Click on this button to view the details of your music

✔	Name	Time	Artist	▲	Album
✔	Digital Booklet – The Suburbs		Arcade Fire		The Suburbs
✔	The Suburbs	5:15	Arcade Fire		The Suburbs
✔	Ready to Start	4:16	Arcade Fire		The Suburbs
✔	Modern Man	4:40	Arcade Fire		The Suburbs
✔	Rococo	3:57	Arcade Fire		The Suburbs
✔	Empty Room	2:52	Arcade Fire		The Suburbs
✔	City With No Children	3:12	Arcade Fire		The Suburbs
✔	Half Light I	4:14	Arcade Fire		The Suburbs

3 Click on this button to view the cover artwork of your music. Swipe with two fingers on the trackpad to move between the covers or use the scroll bar below the covers

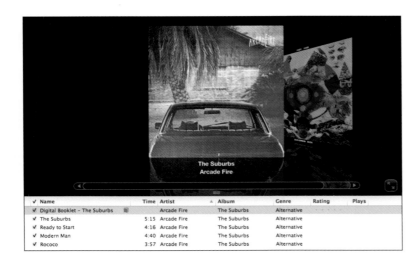

Purchasing Music

As well as copying music from CDs into iTunes, it is also possible to download a vast selection of music from the iTunes online store. To do this:

 Click on the iTunes Store link to access the online store

 Navigate around the iTunes store using the tabs along the top of the iTunes window

 To find a specific item, enter the details in the Search box at the top right-hand corner of the iTunes window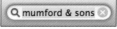

 Details of the item are displayed within the Store

 Click on the Buy Album button to purchase the item.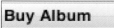

Adding an iPod

Since their introduction in 2001 iPods have become an inescapable part of modern life. It is impossible to sit on a bus or a train without seeing someone with the ubiquitous white earbuds, humming away to their favorite tunes. iPods are for everyone and they are designed to work seamlessly with iTunes; the latter can be used to load music onto the former. To do this:

1 Connect your iPod to the iMac with the supplied USB or Firewire cable

2 iTunes will open automatically and display details about the attached iPod

3 iTunes should automatically start copying music from  the iTunes Library onto the iPod. If not, select the iPod under the Devices heading

4 Select File>Sync from the iTunes Menu bar or click on the Sync button to synchronize iTunes and your iPod

iMovie

For home movie buffs, iMovie offers options for downloading, creating, editing and publishing your efforts:

1 Click on this button on the Dock

2 Attach a digital video camera to your iMac with a Firewire cable

3 Click here to access the camera

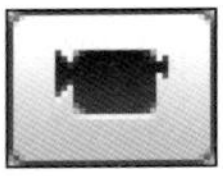

4 Click here to select a camera for

downloading or use the built-in FaceTime one to record your own movie

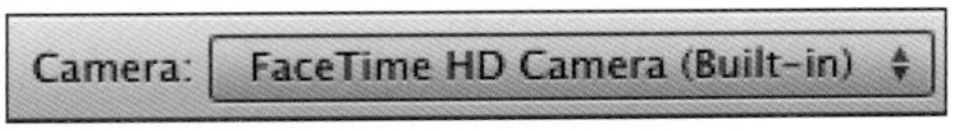

5 Click on the Capture... button to copy the video into iMovie

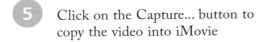

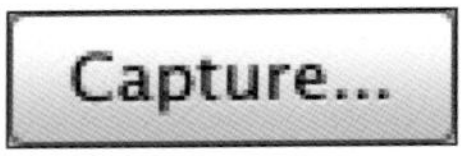

6 Click on the Done button to return to the editing environment

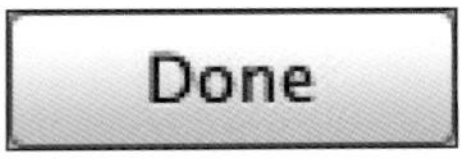

7 Downloaded video clips are shown here

8 Drag a clip into the project window to add it to a new video project

9 Use these buttons to add music, photos, text, transitions and maps to the project

iDVD

Once a video has been created, it can be shared amongst family and friends on a DVD. This can be done through the iDVD app. To do this:

1 Click on this icon on the Dock

2 Click on the Create a New Project option

3 Give the project a name

4 Click on the Create button

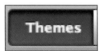

5 Click on the Themes button

6 Click on the Media button to add Audio, Photos and Movies to your iDVD project

7 Click on this button to burn the iDVD project to a DVD

GarageBand

For those who are as interested in creating music as listening to it, GarageBand can be used for this very purpose. It can take a bit of time and practice to become fully proficient with GarageBand but it is worth persevering with if you are musically inclined and want to compose your own. To use GarageBand:

148

1. Click on this icon on the Dock

2. Click on the New Project button

3. Give your new project a name and select a instrument with which to create it

4. Click on this button to start recording

5. Click on the instrument to record the music

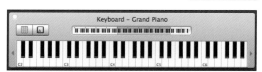

6. Click on this button to view a library of music loops which can be included in your song

7. The song is displayed in the GarageBand timeline

Game Center

Playing games is one of the most popular pastimes on a computer and Mountain Lion gives you ample opportunity to indulge this with the Game Center. To start playing games:

1 Click on this icon in the Launchpad

2 Enter your Apple ID details and click on the Sign In button (or, if you do not have an Apple ID, click on the Create Apple ID button)

3 You can select your own user name and also add a photo for other gamers to see, by clicking on the Change Photo button

4 Click on Games button on the top toolbar

5 Your current games are displayed in the Game Center, including any that you have downloaded on any Apple devices such as iPads, iPhones or iPod Touches

Don't forget

Click on a game to view details about your gaming history and other people's achievements.

Obtaining Games

The Game Center is of little use without games to play and these can be obtained from the App Store. To do this:

1 Within the Game Center, access the Games section as above. Click on this button to find OS X games in the App Store

2 Search for games in the same way as other apps in the App Store

3 Click on a game to download and install it

4 Once a game has been installed, it is available in the Games section of the Game Center. Click on a game to view details about it

5 Click on the Play Game button to open it

10 Sharing OS X

This chapter looks at how to set up different user accounts and how to keep everyone safe on your iMac using parental controls.

Adding Users

OS X enables multiple users to access individual accounts on the same computer. If there are multiple users, i.e. two or more, for a single machine, each person can sign on individually and access their own files and folders. This means that each person can log in to their own settings and preferences. All user accounts can be password protected, to ensure that each user's environment is secure. To set up multiple user accounts:

Don't forget

Every computer with multiple users has at least one main user, also known as an administrator. This means that they have greater control over the number of items that they can edit and alter. If there is only one user on a computer, they automatically take on the role of the administrator. Administrators have a particularly important role to play when computers are networked together. Each computer can potentially have several administrators.

1   Click on the System Preferences icon on the Dock

2   Click on the Users & Groups icon

Users & Groups

3   The information about the current account is displayed. This is your own account and the information is based on details you provided when you first set up your iMac

Don't forget

Each user can select their own icon or photo of themselves.

4   Click on this icon to enable new accounts to be added (the padlock needs to be open)

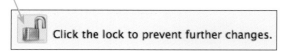

Click the lock to prevent further changes.

5 Click on the plus sign icon to add a new account

6 Enter the details for the new account holder

Don't forget

By default, you are the administrator of your own iMac. This means that you can administer other user accounts.

153

7 Click on the Create User button

Create User

8 The new account is added to the list in the Accounts window, under Other Accounts

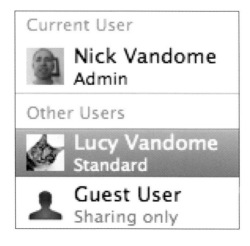

Deleting Users

Once a user has been added, their name appears on the list in the Accounts preference dialog box. It is then possible to edit the details of a particular user or delete them altogether. To do this:

1 Within Users & Groups, select a user from the list

Current User

Nick Vandome
Admin

Other Users

Lucy Vandome
Standard

2 Click here to remove the selected person's user account

3 A warning box appears to check if you really do want to delete the selected user. If you do, select the required option and click on OK

Are you sure you want to delete the user account "Lucy Vandome"?

To delete this user account, select what you want to do with the home folder for this account, and then click OK.

- ● Save the home folder in a disk image
  The disk image is saved in the Deleted Users folder (in the Users folder).
- ○ Don't change the home folder
  The home folder remains in the Users folder.
- ○ Delete the home folder
  ☐ Erase home folder securely

Cancel   OK

Fast User Switching

If there are multiple users using OS X it is useful to be able to switch between them as quickly as possible. When this is done, the first user's session is retained so that they can return to it if required. To switch between users:

1 In the Users & Groups window, click on the Login Options button

2 Check on the Show fast user switching menu box

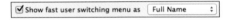

3 At the top-right of the screen, click on the current user's name

Don't forget

When you switch between users, the first user remains logged in and their current session is retained intact.

4 Click on the name of another user

5 Enter the relevant password (if required)

6 Click on this button to login

155

OS X for the Family

Many families share their computers between multiple users and, with the ability to create different accounts in OS X, each user can have their own customized workspace. If desired, you can also set up an Apple ID so that other users can access a wider range of products, such as the Apple App Store. To do this:

1 Access Users & Groups

2 Click on the Apple ID Set... button

3 If the user already has an Apple ID, enter it in the appropriate box. If not click on the Create Apple ID button to create an account

4 A page on the Apple website is accessed. This contains general information about an Apple ID and also a facility for obtaining one

Parental Controls

If children are using the computer, parents may want to restrict access to certain types of information that can be viewed, using Parental Controls. To do this:

1 Access Users & Groups, click on a username then check on the Enable Parental Controls box and click on the Open Parental Controls... button

2 Click on the Apps tab

3 Check on the Use Simple Finder box to show a simplified version of the Finder

4 Check on this box if you want to limit the types of app that a user can access

5 Check off the boxes next to the apps that you do not want to be used

6 Click here to select options for age limits in terms of accessing items in the App Store

Allow App Store Apps: | up to 12+

...cont'd

Web controls

1 Click on the Web tab

2 Check on this button to limit access to websites with adult content

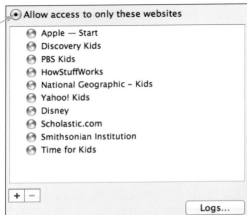

3 Check on this button to define specific websites that are suitable to be viewed

People controls

1 Click on the People tab

2 Check on the Limit boxes to limit the type of content in email messages, games and messages

Time Limits controls

1 Click on the Time Limits tab   **Time Limits**

2 Check on this box to limit the amount of time the user can use the iMac during weekdays

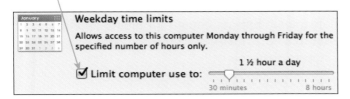

Weekday time limits

Allows access to this computer Monday through Friday for the specified number of hours only.

1 ½ hour a day

☑ Limit computer use to:

30 minutes   8 hours

3 Check on this box to limit the amount of time the user can use the iMac during weekends

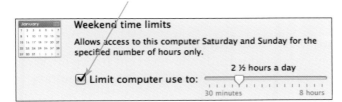

Weekend time limits

Allows access to this computer Saturday and Sunday for the specified number of hours only.

2 ½ hours a day

☑ Limit computer use to:

30 minutes   8 hours

4 Check on these boxes to determine the times at which the user cannot access their account

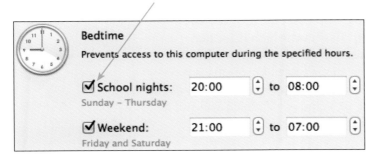

Bedtime

Prevents access to this computer during the specified hours.

☑ School nights: 20:00 ⬍ to 08:00 ⬍
Sunday – Thursday

☑ Weekend: 21:00 ⬍ to 07:00 ⬍
Friday and Saturday

OS X for Windows Users

General sharing

One of the historical complaints about Macs is that it is difficult to share files between them and Microsoft Windows computers. While this may have been true with some file types in years gone by, this is an issue that is becoming less and less important, particularly with OS X. Some of the reasons for this are:

- A number of popular file formats, such as PDFs (Portable Document Format) for documents and JPEGs (Joint Photographic Experts Group) for photos and images, are designed so that they can be used on both Mac and Windows platforms

- A lot of software apps on the iMac have options for saving files into different formats, including ones that are specifically for Windows machines

- Other popular apps, such as Microsoft Office, now have Mac versions and the resulting files can be shared on both formats

Sharing with Boot Camp

For people who find it hard to live without Microsoft Windows, help is at hand even on an iMac. iMacs have an app called Boot Camp that can be used to run a version of Windows on an iMac. This is available with Mountain Lion. Once it has been accessed, a copy of Windows can then be installed and run. This means that if you have a non-Mac app that you want to use on your iMac, you can do so with Boot Camp.

Boot Camp is set up with the Boot Camp Assistant which is located within the Utilities folder within the Applications folder. Once this is run you can then install either Windows XP, Vista or Windows 7 which will run at its native speed.

11 iMac Networking

This chapter looks at how to use your iMac to create and work with networks between other computers for sharing information.

Networking Overview

Before you start sharing files directly between computers, you have to connect them together. This is known as networking and can be done with two computers in the same room, or with thousands of computers in a major corporation. If you are setting up your own small network it will be known in the computing world as a Local Area Network (LAN). When setting up a network there are various pieces of hardware that are initially needed to join all of the required items together. Once this has been done, software settings can be applied for the networked items. Some of the items of hardware that may be required include:

- **A network card**. This is known as a Network Interface Card (NIC); all recent iMacs have them built-in

- **An Ethernet port and Ethernet cable**. This enables you to make the physical connection between devices. Ethernet cables come in a variety of forms, but the one you should be looking for is the Cat5E type as this allows for the fastest transfer of data. If you are creating a wireless network, you will not require these

- **A hub**. This is a piece of hardware with multiple Ethernet ports that enables you to connect all of your devices together and lets them communicate with each other. However, conflicts can occur with hubs if two devices try to send data through it at the same time

- **A switch**. This is similar in operation to a hub but is more sophisticated in its method of data transfer, thus allowing all of the machines on the network to communicate simultaneously, unlike a hub

Once you have worked out all of the devices you want to include on your network you can arrange them accordingly. Try to keep the switches and hub within relative proximity of a power supply and, if you are using cables, make sure they are laid out safely.

It is perfectly possible to create a simple network of two computers just by joining them with an Ethernet cable.

Ethernet network

The cheapest and easiest way to network computers is to create an Ethernet network. This involves buying an Ethernet hub or switch, which enables you to connect several devices to a central point, i.e. the hub or switch. All iMacs, and most modern printers, have an Ethernet port, so it is possible to connect various devices, not just computers. Once all of the devices have been connected by Ethernet cables, you can then start applying network settings.

AirPort network

The other option for creating a network is an AirPort network. This is a wireless network and there are two main standards used by Apple computers: AirPort, using the IEEE 802.11b standard, which is more commonly known as Wi-Fi, which stands for Wireless Fidelity, and the newer AirPort Extreme, using the newer IEEE 802.11g standard, which is up to 5 times faster than the older 802.11b standard. Thankfully, AirPort Extreme is also compatible with devices based on the older standard, so one machine loaded with AirPort Extreme can still communicate wirelessly with an older AirPort one.

One of the issues with a wireless network is security, since it is possible for someone with a wireless-enabled machine to access your wireless network, if they are within range. However, in the majority of cases, the chances of this happening are fairly slim, although it is an issue you should be aware of.

The basics of a wireless network with iMacs is an AirPort card (either AirPort or AirPort Extreme) installed in all of the required machines, and an AirPort base station that can be located anywhere within 150 m of the AirPort-enabled computers. Once the hardware is in place, wireless-enabled devices can be configured by using the AirPort Setup Assistant utility found in the Utilities folder. After AirPort has been set up, the wireless network can be connected. All of the wireless-enabled devices should then be able to communicate with each other, without using a multitude of cables.

Don't forget

Another method for connecting items wirelessly is called Bluetooth. This covers much shorter distances than AirPort and is generally used for items like printers and cellphones. Bluetooth devices can be connected by using the Bluetooth Setup Assistant in the Utilities folder.

Network Settings

Once you have connected the hardware required for a network, you can start applying the network settings that are required for different computers to communicate with one another. To network two iMac computers):

1 In System Preferences, click on the Network button

2 For a wireless connection, click on the Turn Wi-Fi On button

3 Details of wireless settings are displayed

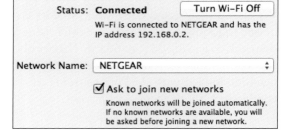

4 For a cable connection, connect an Ethernet cable

5 Details of the cable settings are displayed

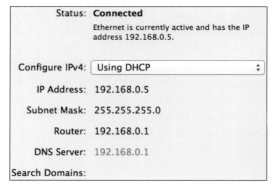

6 Click on the Advanced... button to see the full settings for each option

Network Preferences

Before you can share files on a network, or access the Internet, the appropriate network settings have to be applied on your iMac so that the network is prepared. This is done by creating a new named network. To do this:

1 In System Preferences, double-click on the Network icon

2 Network details are displayed in the same way as for connecting to the Internet (as shown in Chapter Eight)

3 If you are already connected to a network, this will be shown in the Status section. If you are connected to a wireless network the connection will be via Airport

Beware

If you turn off the Wi-Fi function, this will disconnect you from your network and also the Internet.

> **Status: Connected**   **Turn Wi-Fi Off**
>
> Wi-Fi is connected to NETGEAR and has the IP address 192.168.0.3.

4 The network name is shown here

> **Network Name:**   NETGEAR

...cont'd

5 Check this box if you want to be notified before joining a new network

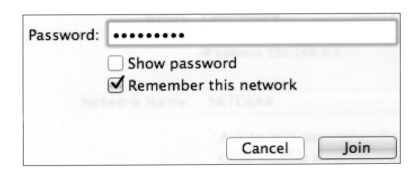
☑ **Ask to join new networks**
Known networks will be joined automatically. If no known networks are available, you will be asked before joining a new network.

6 Click on the Advanced... button to access a range of options for both Wi-Fi and cable network connections

Advanced...

Don't forget

If you are asked to join new networks, all of the available networks in range will be displayed, not just the one you may want to join.

166

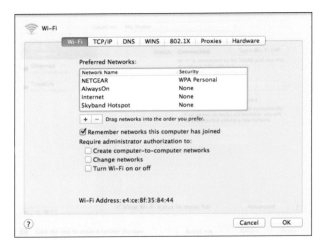

7 If you join a new network you may be asked to enter a password for the network (this is a security measure for the router that provides the network). Click on the Join button

Password: ●●●●●●●●●
☐ Show password
☑ Remember this network

Cancel   Join

Network Diagnostics

If your network is unavailable you can check to see what the problem is. To do this:

1 If you cannot connect to the Internet, Safari will return to a page with this button on it. Click on it to try to find the problem

Network Diagnostics...

2 Select the network name you are using

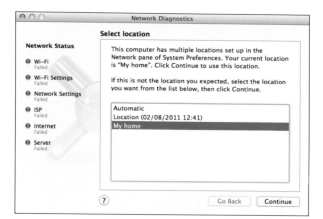

167

Hot tip

Over time, you may end up with a number of network names, not all of which are still used. Delete any names that are redundant so that the list does not become too long.

3 Click on the Continue button

Continue

4 The status of the network is shown in the left-hand panel. Select the method you want to connect to a network with, e.g. Wi-Fi (wireless). Click on the Continue button

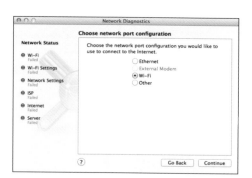

...cont'd

5 Wi-Fi needs to be turned on for the network diagnostics to continue

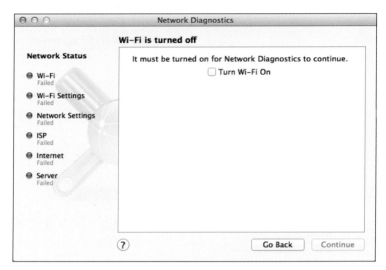

6 Check the Turn Wi-Fi On box and click the Continue button

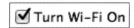

7 Select an available network. The left-hand panel will display the status for each required element

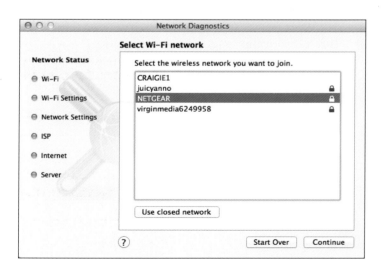

Connecting to a Network

Connecting as a registered user

To connect as a registered user (usually as yourself when you want to access items on another one of your own computers):

1 Other connected computers on the network will show up in the Shared section in the Finder. Click on a networked computer

2 Click on the Connect As... button

3 Check on the Registered User button and enter your username and password

Don't forget

Your username and password are specified in the Accounts section of System Preferences.

169

4 Click on the Connect button

5 The hard drive and home folder of the networked computer is available to the registered user. Double-click on an item to view its contents

Don't forget

You can disconnect from a networked computer by ejecting it in the Finder, in the same way as you would a removable drive, such as a DVD.

...cont'd

Guest users

Guest users on a network are users other than yourself, or other registered users, to whom you want to limit access to your files and folders. Guests only have access to a folder called the Drop Box in your own Public folder. To share files with Guest users, you have to first copy them into the Drop Box. To do this:

170

1 Create a file and select File>Save from the Menu bar

2 Navigate to your own home folder (this is created automatically by OS X and is displayed in the Finder Sidebar)

3 Double-click on the Public folder

4 Double-click on the Drop Box folder

5 Save the file into the Drop Box

Accessing a Drop Box

To access files in a Drop Box:

1 Double-click on a networked computer in the Finder

2 Click on the Connect As... button in the Finder window

3 Select the Guest button

It is better to copy files into the Drop Box rather than moving them from their current location completely.

4 Click on the Connect button

Connect

5 Double-click on the administrator's home folder

Hot tip

Set permissions for how the Drop Box operates by selecting it in the Finder and Ctrl+clicking on it. Select Get Info from the menu and apply the required settings under the Ownership & Permissions heading.

6 Double-click on the Drop Box folder to access the files within it

File Sharing

One of the main reasons for creating a network of two or more computers is to share files between them. On networked iMacs, this involves setting them up so that they can share files and then accessing these files.

Setting up file sharing

To set up file sharing on a networked iMac:

1 Click on the System Preferences icon on the Dock

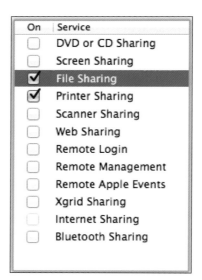

2 Click on the Sharing icon

3 Check the boxes next to the items you want to share (the most common items to share are files and printers)

On	Service
☐	DVD or CD Sharing
☐	Screen Sharing
☑	File Sharing
☑	Printer Sharing
☐	Scanner Sharing
☐	Web Sharing
☐	Remote Login
☐	Remote Management
☐	Remote Apple Events
☐	Xgrid Sharing
☐	Internet Sharing
☐	Bluetooth Sharing

4 Click on the padlock to close it and prevent more changes

12 iMac Maintenance

Despite its stability, OS X still benefits from a robust maintenance regime. This chapter looks at ways to keep OS X in top shape and some general troubleshooting.

Time Machine

Time Machine is a feature of OS X that gives you great peace of mind. In conjunction with an external hard drive, it creates a backup of your whole system, including folders, files, apps and even the OS X operating system itself.

Once it has been set up, Time Machine takes a backup every hour and you can then go into Time Machine to restore any files that have been deleted or become corrupt.

Setting up Time Machine

To use Time Machine it has to first be set up. This involves attaching a hard drive to your iMac. To set up Time Machine:

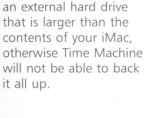

Beware

Make sure that you have an external hard drive that is larger than the contents of your iMac, otherwise Time Machine will not be able to back it all up.

1   Click on the Time Machine icon on the Dock or access it in the System Preferences

2   You will be prompted to set up Time Machine

3   Click on the Set Up Time Machine button

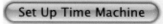

4   In the Time Machine System Preferences window, click on the Choose Backup Disk... button

5 Connect an external hard drive and select it

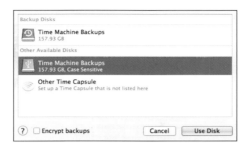

6 Click on the Use for Backup button

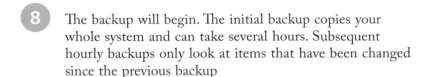

7 In the Time Machine System Preferences window, drag the button to the On position

8 The backup will begin. The initial backup copies your whole system and can take several hours. Subsequent hourly backups only look at items that have been changed since the previous backup

9 The progress of the backup is displayed in the System Preferences window and also here

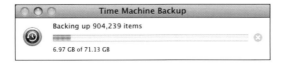

Beware

When you first set up Time Machine it copies everything on your iMac. Depending on the type of connection you have for your external drive, this could take several hours, or even days. Because of this it is a good idea to have a hard drive with a FireWire connection to make it as fast as possible.

Don't forget

If you stop the initial backup before it has been completed Time Machine will remember where it has stopped and resume the backup from this point.

...cont'd

Using Time Machine

Once the Time Machine has been set up it can then be used to go back in time to view items in an earlier state. To do this:

1 Access an item on your iMac and delete it. In this example IMG_2137 is deleted

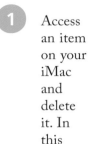

2 Click on the Time Machine icon on the Dock

3 The Time Machine displays the current item in its current state (the image is deleted). Earlier versions are stacked behind it

4 Click on the arrows to move through the open items or select a time or date from the scale to the right of the arrows

5 Another way to move through the Time Machine is to click on the pages behind the front one. This brings the selected item to the front. In this example, Time Machine has gone back to a date when the image was still in place, i.e. before it was deleted

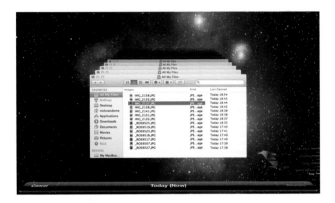

Don't forget

Items are restored from the Time Machine backup disk, i.e. the external hard drive.

6 Click on the Restore button to restore the item that has been deleted

7 Click on the Cancel button to return to your normal environment

8 The deleted image is now restored in its original location

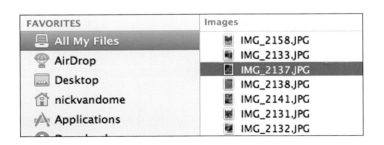

Disk Utility

Disk Utility is a utility app that allows you to perform certain testing and repair functions for OS X. It incorporates a variety of functions and it is a good option for general maintenance and if your computer is not running as it should.

Each of the functions within Disk Utility can be applied to specific drives and volumes. However, it is not possible to use the OS X start-up disk within Disk Utility as this will be in operation to run the app and Disk Utility cannot operate on a disk that has apps already running. To use Disk Utility:

Checking disks

Don't forget

Disk Utility is located within the Applications> Utilities folder.

Don't forget

If there is a problem with a disk and OS X can fix it, the Repair button will be available. Click on this to enable Disk Utility to repair the problem.

1 Click the First Aid tab to check a disk

2 Select a disk and select one of the first aid options

Erasing a disk
To erase all of the data on a disk or a volume:

1 Click on the Erase tab and select a disk or a volume

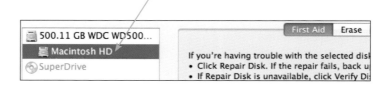

Beware

If you erase data from a removable disk, such as a pen drive, you will not be able to retrieve it.

2 Click Erase to erase the data on the selected disk or volume

System Information

This can be used to view how the different hardware and software elements on your iMac are performing. To do this:

1 Open the Utilities folder and double-click on the System Information icon

2 Click on the Hardware link and click on an item of hardware

▼ Hardware
 ATA
 Audio (Built In)
 Bluetooth
 Card Reader
 Diagnostics
 Disc Burning

Don't forget

System Information is located within the Applications>Utilities folder.

179

3 Details about the item of hardware, and its performance, are displayed

```
OPTIARC DVD RW AD-5690H:

Firmware Revision:  4AH5
Interconnect:       ATAPI
Burn Support:       Yes (Apple Shipping Drive)
Cache:              2048 KB
Reads DVD:          Yes
CD-Write:           -R, -RW
DVD-Write:          -R, -R DL, -RW, +R, +R DL, +RW
Write Strategies:   CD-TAO, CD-SAO, CD-Raw, DVD-DAO
Media:              To show the available burn speeds, insert a disc and
                    choose View > Refresh
```

4 Click on software items to view their details

```
iMovie                      9.0.4        11/07/2011 19:3
IncompatibleAppDisplay      400          11/11/2011 13:0

iMovie:

Version:         9.0.4
Last Modified:   11/07/2011 19:31
Kind:            Intel
64-Bit (Intel):  No
App Store:       No
Get Info String: 9.0.4, Copyright © 1999-2001, 2003-2011 Apple Inc. All
                 rights reserved.
Location:        /Applications/iMovie.app
```

Activity Monitor

Activity Monitor is a utility app that can be used to view information about how much processing power and memory are being used to run apps. This can be useful to know if certain apps are running slowly or crashing frequently. To use Activity Monitor:

Don't forget

Activity Monitor is located within the Applications>Utilities folder.

1 Click on the CPU tab to see how much processor memory is being used up

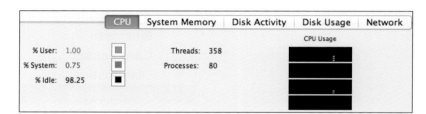

2 Click on the System Memory tab to see how much system memory (RAM) is being used up

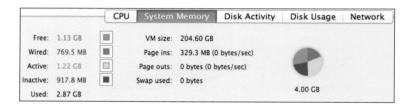

3 Click on the Disk Usage tab to see how much space has been taken up on the hard drive

Updating Software

Apple periodically releases updates for its software, for both its apps and the OS X operating system. All of these are now available through the App Store. To update software:

1 Open System Preferences and click on the Software Update icon

Software Update

2 Click here to select options for how you are notified about updates and how they are downloaded

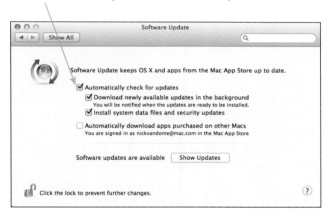

181

3 If updates are available, click on the Show Updates button

Software updates are available   Show Updates

4 Available updates are shown in the Updates section in the App Store. Click on the Update buttons to update

Gatekeeper

Internet security is an important issue for every computer user; no-one wants their computer to be infected with a virus or malicious software. Historically, Macs have been less prone to attack from viruses than Windows-based machines, but this does not mean Mac users can be complacent. With their increasing popularity there is now more temptation for virus writers to target them. Mountain Lion recognizes this and has taken steps to prevent attacks with the Gatekeeper function. To use this:

1 Open System Preferences and click on the Security & Privacy button

Security & Privacy

2 Click on the General tab 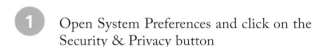 General

3 Click on these buttons to determine which apps can be downloaded. Before Mountain Lion, apps were downloaded from anywhere. Now you can select to also only have them from just the App Store, or the App Store and identified developers, which gives you added security in terms of apps having been thoroughly checked

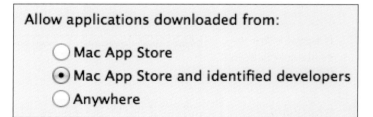

Allow applications downloaded from:

○ Mac App Store
◉ Mac App Store and identified developers
○ Anywhere

4 Under the General tab there are also options for using a password when you login to your account and also if a password is required after sleep or the screen saver

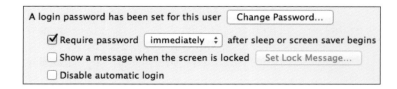

A login password has been set for this user [Change Password...]

☑ Require password [immediately ⇕] after sleep or screen saver begins
☐ Show a message when the screen is locked [Set Lock Message...]
☐ Disable automatic login

Privacy

Also within the Security & Privacy System Preferences are options for activating a firewall and privacy settings:

1 Click on the Firewall tab

2 Click on the Turn On Firewall button to activate this

3 Click on the Privacy tab

4 Click on the Location Services link and check On the Enable Location Services if you want relevant apps to be able to access your location

5 Click on the Contacts link and check On any relevant apps that want to access your Contacts

6 Click on the Diagnostics & Usage link and check On the Send diagnostic & usage data to Apple if you want to send information to Apple about the performance of your iMac and its apps. This will include any problems and helps Apple improve its software and apps. This information is collected anonymously and does not identify anyone personally

Don't forget

Mountain Lion apps are designed to do only what they are supposed to, so that they do not have to interact with other apps if they do not need to. This lessens the possibility of any viruses spreading across your iMac. For instance, only apps that can use Contacts will ask for permission to do this.

Problems with Apps

The simple answer

OS X is something of a rarity in the world of computing software; it claims to be remarkably stable, and it is. However, this is not to say that things do not sometimes go wrong, although this is considerably less frequent than with older Mac operating systems. Sometimes this will be due to problems within particular apps and on occasions the problems may lie with OS X itself. If this does happen, the first course of action is to close down OS X using the Apple menu>Shut Down command. Then, restart the computer. If this does not work, or you cannot access the Shut Down command, try turning off the power to the computer and then starting up again.

Force quitting

If a particular app is not responding it can be closed down separately without the need to reboot the computer. To do this:

1 Select Apple menu>Force Quit from the Menu bar

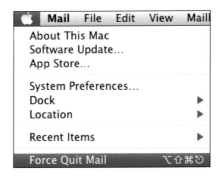

2 Select the app you want to close

3 Click Force Quit

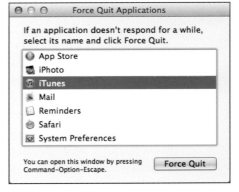

General Troubleshooting

It is true that things do go wrong with OS X, although probably with less regularity than with some other operating systems. If something does go wrong, there are a number of items that you can check and also some steps you can take to ensure that you do not lose any important data if the worst-case scenario occurs and your hard drive packs up completely.

- **Backup**. If everything does go wrong it is essential to take preventative action in the form of making sure that all of your data is backed up and saved. This can either be done with the Time Machine app or by backing up manually by copying data to a CD or DVD

- **Reboot**. One traditional reply by IT helpdesks is to reboot, i.e. turn off the computer and turn it back on again, and hope that the problem has resolved itself. In a lot of cases this simple operation does the trick but it is not always a viable solution for major problems

- **Check cables**. If the problem appears to be with a network connection or an externally-connected device, check that all cables are connected properly and have not worked loose. If possible, make sure that all cables are tucked away so that they cannot be pulled out by accident

- **Check network settings**. If your network or Internet connections are not working, check the network setting in System Preferences. Sometimes when you make a change to one item this can have an adverse effect on one of these settings. (If possible, lock the settings once you have applied them, by clicking on the padlock icon in the Network preferences window.)

- **Check for viruses**. If your computer is infected with a virus this could affect the efficient running of the machine. Luckily this is less of a problem for Macs as virus writers tend to concentrate their efforts towards Windows-based machines. However, there are plenty of Mac viruses out there, so make sure your computer is protected by an app such as Norton AntiVirus which is available from www.symantec.com

Don't forget

In extreme cases, you will not be able to reboot your computer normally. If this happens, you will have to pull out the power cable and reattach it. You will then be able to reboot, although the computer may want to check its hard drive to make sure that everything is in working order.

...cont'd

- **Check Start-up items**. If you have set certain items to start automatically when your computer is turned on, this could cause certain conflicts within your machine. If this is the case, disable the items from launching during the booting up of the computer. This can be done within the Accounts preference of System Preferences by clicking on the Startup Items tab, selecting the relevant item and pressing the minus button

- **Check permissions**. If you, or other users, are having problems opening items this could be because of the permissions that are set. To check these, select the item in the Finder, click on the File button on the Finder toolbar and select Get Info. In the Ownership & Permissions section of the Info window you will be able to set the relevant permissions to allow other users, or yourself, to read, write or have no access

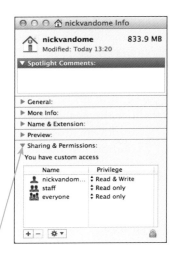

Click here to view permissions settings

- **Eject external devices**. Sometimes external devices, such as pen drives, can become temperamental and refuse to eject the disks within them, or even show up on the desktop or in the Finder. If this happens you can eject the disk by pressing the mouse button when the Mac chimes are heard during the booting up process

- **Turn off your screen saver**. Screen savers can sometimes cause conflicts within your computer, particularly if they have been downloaded from an unreliable source. If this happens, change the screen saver within the Desktop & Screen Saver preference of the System Preferences or disable it altogether

Index